**THOMAS BUERGENTHAL** has dedicated his life to international law and the protection of human rights. He has combined a career as a professor of international law with judicial positions and investigatory activities relating to international human rights and the rule of law.

Buergenthal served as the American judge on the International Court of Justice in The Hague from 2000 to 2010. On his return to the United States, he was reappointed Lobingier Professor of Comparative Law and Jurisprudence by the George Washington University Law School in Washington DC, a position he had held from 1989 until his election to the ICJ.

Buergenthal's academic career began at the State University of New York at Buffalo Law School in 1962. There followed appointments as Fulbright & Jaworski Professor at the University of Texas Law School in Austin; Dean of the Washington College of Law of the American University, Washington DC;

I.T. Cohen Professor of Human Rights at the Emory University Law School; and Director of the Human Rights Programme of the Carter Center in Atlanta, Georgia.

Prior to his election to the ICJ, Buergenthal served as judge and president of the Inter-American Court of Human Rights as well as judge and president of the Administrative Tribunal of the Inter-American Development Bank. He was a member of the UN Human Rights Committee and the UN Truth Commission for El Salvador, and served as chairman of the Committee of Conscience of the US Holocaust Memorial Museum and vice chairman of the Claims Resolution Tribunal for Dormant Accounts in Switzerland. He is a member of the Ethics Commission of the International Olympic Committee and honorary president of the Inter-American Institute of Human Rights.

Buergenthal graduated from Bethany College, West Virginia. He earned his Juris Doctor degree from New York University School of Law, and his Master of Laws and Doctor of Juridical Science degrees from Harvard Law School. He has received more than a dozen honorary doctorates from universities in the US, Europe and Latin America.

He is a recipient of the American Society of International Law 2002 Manley O. Hudson Award; the Gruber Foundation 2008 Justice Prize; and the US Holocaust Memorial Museum 2015 Elie Wiesel Prize. Buergenthal and his wife, Peggy, live in the Washington DC area.

'There is a contrast between the horrors Buergenthal recounts and the positive tone of his memoir. He has waited more than fifty years to write *A Lucky Child*, and it is the detachment of distance, coupled with the author's gracious spirit, that steers the prose away from self-pity or anger ... It is what makes this memoir so rewarding: in the darkness, the indomitable spirit of the child' Genevieve Fox, *Telegraph*

'Passionate and objective' Harry McGrath, *Sunday Herald*

'A tour de force: simply narrated, at times almost naive – and even more shocking as a result' Camilla Long, *Sunday Times*

'What Thomas Buergenthal has to say, both in bearing witness to the Holocaust and in describing his moral coming-to-adulthood, deserves our attention. He has serious things to tell us about forgiveness, justice and the curious effect of deep trauma on the mind. His is an extraordinary story and he tells it straight.' Sam Leith, *Daily Mail*

'A book that just has to be read' Pam Norfolk, *Lancashire Evening Post*

'In the plainest words and the steadiest tones Thomas Buergenthal delivers to us the child he once was: an unblemished little boy made human prey by Europe's indelible twentieth-century barbarism. History and memory fail to ebb; rather, they accelerate and proliferate, and Buergenthal's voice is now more thunderous than ever. Pledged to universal human rights, he has turned a life of gratuitous deliverance into a work of visionary compassion.' Cynthia Ozick, author of *The Bear Boy*

'An extraordinary and inspiring book by an extraordinary and inspiring man. It's one of those rare books you devour cover to cover in a single reading. It deserves to be read very widely indeed, especially for anyone desperate for a hint of light in a world that can often seem so very dark.' Professor Philippe Sands QC

'It's a unique, almost magical story – the little boy is like a Kobold or goblin – or some wily younger son in a story by the Brothers Grimm. He survives by a mixture of cunning and sheer dumb luck – he experiences utter horror, but also extraordinary kindness and compassion. This book is also about the getting of wisdom, and young Tommy's determination not to let his dreadful experiences crush his essential humanity.' Kate Saunders

'Wonderful' Phil Bloomfield, *Oxford Times*

'A painfully honest work' Steve Andrew, *Morning Star*

'Thomas Buergenthal is now a distinguished judge at the International Court in The Hague ... this book tells his remarkable story ... the world can learn from this modest, talented and inspiring man.' *Good Book Guide*

'A deeply moving story ... a vivid juxtaposition of matter-of-fact details of the life of a young child and the ultimate horror of a death camp.' Juliet Gardiner, *History Today*

'As understated and optimistic as it is harrowing' Christopher Hart, *Sunday Times*

# A LUCKY CHILD

Thomas Buergenthal at the age of three in Lubochna

# A Lucky
# Child

## A MEMOIR OF SURVIVING
## AUSCHWITZ AS A YOUNG BOY

THOMAS BUERGENTHAL

with a foreword by
ELIE WIESEL

PROFILE BOOKS

This paperback edition published in 2015

First published in Great Britain in 2009 by
PROFILE BOOKS LTD
3 Holford Yard
Bevin Way
London WC1X 9HD
www.profilebooks.com

First published in translation by Fischer Verlag, Germany,
as Ein Glückskind, 2007

1 3 5 7 9 10 8 6 4 2

Typeset in Quadraat by MacGuru Ltd
info@macguru.org.uk
Printed and bound by CPI Group (UK) Ltd, Croydon, CR0 4YY

The moral right of the author has been asserted.

A CIP catalogue record for this book is available from the British Library.

ISBN 978 1 78125 400 4
eISBN 978 1 84765 184 6

MIX
Paper from
responsible sources
FSC® C020471
FSC
www.fsc.org

Dedicated to the memory of my parents, Mundek and Gerda Buergenthal, whose love, strength of character and integrity inspired this book

# Contents

Map      xii

Foreword by Elie Wiesel      xv

Preface      xxi

Chapter 1: From Lubochna to Poland      1

Chapter 2: Katowice      24

Chapter 3: The Ghetto of Kielce      37

Chapter 4: Auschwitz      64

Chapter 5: The Auschwitz Death Transport      88

Chapter 6: Liberation      99

Chapter 7: Into the Polish Army      117

Chapter 8: Waiting to Be Found      134

Chapter 9: A New Beginning      154

Chapter 10: Life in Germany      166

Chapter 11: To America      197

Epilogue      211

Afterword      230

Acknowledgements      261

# Foreword

Are there rules to help a survivor decide the best time to bear witness to history? Which is better: to dare to look directly into the blinding present, no matter how painful, or, to await the detachment of hindsight – which, being less painful, is more objective?

In the literature of what we so inadequately call the Holocaust, there were prisoners who, possessed by the fear of oblivion, defied every danger by becoming chroniclers. In the ghettos and in the death camps, and even in the shadow of the flames of Birkenau and Treblinka, men scrounged paper and pencil to write down and preserve their daily existence in all its appalling horror. These precious documents were discovered buried in the ground or under mountains of ash.

Following the war and shortly after their liberation from Auschwitz or Buchenwald, some survivors felt the need to speak out. The world had to be told the truth – not only about their suffering but also about its own treachery. Others held their tongues, mostly because they did not have the strength to relive events that had been just about unbearable. And then too, let us be honest, people preferred not to hear what they had to say. It prevented them from clinging to their own certainties or, more simply, from eating well and sleeping in peace.

Thomas Buergenthal is among those who chose to wait. In his case, the long delay has been rich in human experience. He was already at the height of his career as a professor of law and as a judge before an international court when he decided to revisit his memories.

Is his testimony just one among many, similar to so many others? Well, yes and no. At first glance, all accounts seem to tell the same story. Sometimes we may even wonder whether it was the same German tormenter who abused, tortured, and killed the same Jew six million times. And yet, each story retains its own identity, its own voice.

The voice of the future world court judge strikes us by its need to seek out strains of humanity, even in the very depths of hell.

Kielce, Henryków, Birkenau, Gliwice and Sachsenhausen – Buergenthal was among the youngest of prisoners in all these places of pain and damnation, where the power of evil and death seemed absolute. Being a mere ten years old in Birkenau made him a rarity, if not almost unique. How did he escape the brutality of the bosses, the agonies of hunger, the fatal diseases, and the selections? More simply put, how did he survive? If he believed in God, he might have evoked divine intervention, but he attributes his survival to luck. As a matter of fact, a clairvoyant had predicted as much to his mother: her son would be lucky. He remembers her saying so.

In the beginning there was the ghetto, with its famished wraiths, its nights of fear, its defeats; profession, wealth, and lineage counted for nothing there. Inside the primal nightmare, a most orderly chaos.

Then, deportation: the nocturnal passage into the unknown. Was it simply by chance that Thomas avoided the scrutiny of the infamous Doctor Mengele upon his arrival at Birkenau? Was there a tangible explanation for his luck? On another occasion, during a selection, the boy was bold enough to announce in German to a commandant that he could work. Amazingly, the commandant pulled him from the group destined for death. Other boys his age had already gone to 'the other place,' up there in the clouds, whereas he, Thomas, was still alive. One day, he was astonished to catch a glimpse of his mother in the women's camp.

How can those who have never been put to the test understand how human nature may bend under duress? Why does one man become a pitiless Kapo and victimise an old friend or even his own relative? What makes one man choose to exercise power through cruelty, while another – from exactly the same background – refuses to do so in the name of enfeebled and downtrodden humanity?

Thomas watches, learns, and remembers. Firing squads. Hangings. The prisoner who, not wishing to lose his dignity, kisses the hand of the unfortunate friend condemned to serve as his executioner.

In fact, even in the terrible camp at Sachsenhausen, Thomas

finds friends – older than him, men from his own district or from faraway places like Norway – who help him.

Thomas's stories from the days following liberation resemble earlier accounts in their thirst to understand what man, pushed to the very limits, is capable of.

As a child in Göttingen, Germany, he dreamed of going out onto the balcony with a machine gun in his hand to seek vengeance. Later, that dream shamed and humbled him. The same townsmen who, under Hitler, had turned their backs on their Jewish neighbours now embrace them. And Thomas, who has come to Göttingen to be with his mother, does not judge them collectively guilty.

Would he have written the same book fifty years ago? There is no knowing. But he has written it. That alone is what matters. And for it the reader must surely be thankful to him.

Elie Wiesel

# A Lucky Child

# Preface

This book should probably have been written many years ago, when the events I describe were still fresh in my mind. But my other life intervened – the life I have lived since I arrived in the United States in 1951, a life filled with educational, professional and family responsibilities that left little time for the past. It may be also that I needed the distance of more than half a century to record my earlier life, for it allowed me to examine my childhood experiences with greater detachment and without dwelling on many details that are not really central to the story I now believe it is important to tell. That story, after all, continues to have a lasting impact on the person I have become.

Of course, I always knew that some day I would have to tell it to my children and then my grandchildren. I believe it is important for them to know what it was like to be a child in the Holocaust and to have survived the concentration camps. My children had heard snippets of my story at the dinner table and family gatherings, but never the whole story. Mine is not, after all, a story that lends itself to such occasional telling. But it is a story that must be told and passed on, particularly in a family that was for all practical purposes wiped out in the Holocaust. Only thus can the link between the past and the future be re-established for our family. For example I have never really managed to tell my children, in its proper context, about the strength of character displayed by their grandparents at a time when other people in similar circumstances lost their moral compass completely. Their courage and integrity enrich the history of our family, and must not be buried with me.

I also wanted to present my story to a wider audience, not because I think that my early life was especially noteworthy in the greater scheme of things, but because I have long believed that the Holocaust cannot be fully understood unless viewed through the eyes of those who lived through it. To speak of the Holocaust in terms of a number – 6 million – which is the way it is usually done, is unintentionally to dehumanise the victims and to trivialise the profoundly human tragedy it was. The number transforms the victims into a fungible mass of name-less, soulless bodies rather than the individuals they were. Each of us who lived through the Holocaust has a personal story worth telling, if only because it puts a human face on the experience. Like all tragedies, the Holocaust produced its heroes and villains, ordinary human beings who never lost their humanity and those who, to save themselves or for a mere piece of bread, helped send others to the gas chambers. It is also the story of some Germans who, in the midst of the car-nage, did not lose their humanity.

For me, the individual story of each survivor is a valuable addition to the Holocaust's history. It deepens our understanding of this cataclysmic event that destroyed for ever not only European Jewry as such, but also its unique culture and character. That is why I have tried to write my own account from the perspective of the child I was, not as an old man reflecting on that life, and to retain its character as the contemporaneous personal testimony of one child-survivor.

This book contains my recollections of events that took place more than six decades ago. These recollections are, I am sure, coloured by the tricks that the passage of time and old age play on memory: forgotten or inaccurate names of people; muddled facts and dates of events that took place either earlier or later than recounted; and references to events that did not happen quite as I describe them or that I believe I witnessed, but may only have heard about. Because I did not write this book earlier, I could no longer consult those who were with me in the camps and compare my recollections of specific events with theirs, and I regret that very much. Most of all I regret that I could not discuss the details with my mother. Also, despite my best efforts, I have found it difficult, if not impossible, particularly in the book's first two chapters, to distinguish clearly between some events I actually remember witnessing and those I was told about by my parents or overheard them discuss. All I can say is that as I wrote about them, I seemed to remember them clearly as first-hand experiences.

Similarly, although the chapters are organised in

chronological order, the episodes within them may not be. After all these years, I can recall particular events or episodes, frequently very clearly, but not exactly when they occurred. To the child I was, dates or time had little significance. As I try to recall that period of my life, I realise that I did not think in terms of days, months or even years, as I would today. I grew up in the camps, I knew no other life, and my sole objective was to stay alive, from hour to hour, from day to day. That was my mindset. I measured time only in terms of the hours we had to wait to receive our next meal or the days remaining before Dr Mengele would mount another of his deadly selections. For example when I began writing I had no idea in which month of 1944 I arrived in Auschwitz. (I obtained that information only after consulting the Auschwitz archives.) The internet provided me with the date of my liberation from Sachsenhausen and that of the liquidation of the ghetto of Kielce. This is the extent of my research; the rest of the story is based on my own recollections.

Had I written this book in the mid-1950s, when I made a first attempt to tell part of my story by publishing an account of the Auschwitz Death March in a college literary magazine, this memoir would have conveyed a greater sense of immediacy to the events I describe. Back then, unencumbered by the mellowing impact that the passage of time has on memory, particularly painful memories, I could still vividly recall my fear of dying, the hunger I experienced, the sense of loss and insecurity that gripped me on being separated from my parents, and my reactions to the horrors I witnessed. Time and the life I have lived since then have dulled those feelings and emotions. As an author I regret that, for I am sure the reader would have been interested in that side of the story as well. But I am convinced that if these feelings and emotions had not lost some of their intensity over the years I would have found it difficult, if not impossible, to overcome my past without serious psychological scarring. It may have been my salvation that these memories faded over time.

My childhood experience has had a substantial impact on the human being I have become, on my life as an international law professor, human rights lawyer and international judge. It might seem obvious that my past would draw me to human rights and to international law, whether or not I knew it at the time. In any event, it equipped me to be a better human rights lawyer, if only because I understood, not only intellectually but also emotionally, what it is like to be a victim of human rights violations. I could, after all, feel it in my bones.

# Chapter 1

# From Lubochna to Poland

It was January 1945. Our open railcars offered little protection against the cold, the wind and the snow so typical of the harsh winters of eastern Europe. We were crossing Czechoslovakia on our way from Auschwitz in Poland to the Sachsenhausen concentration camp in Germany. As our train approached a bridge spanning the tracks I saw people waving from the parapet and then, suddenly, loaves of bread came raining down on us. The bread kept coming as we passed under one or two more bridges. Except for snow, I had eaten nothing since we had boarded the train at the end of a three-day forced march out of Auschwitz, only a few days ahead of the advancing Soviet troops. The bread probably saved my life and the lives of many others who were with me on what came to be known as the Auschwitz Death Transport.

At the time, it did not occur to me to connect the bread from the bridges with Czechoslovakia, the country of my birth. That came years after the war, usually recalled on those occasions when, for one reason or another, I was asked to present a birth certificate. Since I did not have one, I would be required to provide an affidavit, attesting, 'on information and belief', that I was born in Lubochna, Czechoslovakia, on 11 May 1934. Whenever I signed one of these documents, I would invariably have a flashback to those Czech bridges.

In the early 1990s, not long after the communist regime collapsed in Czechoslovakia, I finally managed to obtain my birth certificate. It confirmed what I had claimed in my many affidavits and provided the impetus for a visit by my wife Peggy and me to Lubochna, she out of curiosity to see where I was born and I in order to connect with that one piece of land on earth where I first opened my eyes.

We reached Lubochna, a small resort town in the lower Tatra mountains in today's Slovakia, after driving from Bratislava, the capital, for a few hours on winding roads alongside noisy brooks and meandering rivers. By chance, we arrived in Lubochna in May 1991, almost fifty-seven years to the day after my birth there. A beautifully sunny morning greeted us as we drove into this small town surrounded by inviting, mellow mountains which distinguish the lower Tatras from the harsher High Tatras.

Now I understood why my father had dreamed of one day coming back to Lubochna and why my mother had loved it here. It seemed such an idyllic place. As Peggy and I walked through the streets in the hope of finding what used to be my parents' hotel, I realised that, although the official-looking piece of paper I had would forever link me to Lubochna, nothing else did. We never found the hotel – I later learned that it had been demolished some time in the 1960s. Although my visit confirmed to me that Lubochna was truly the beautiful place my parents frequently talked about, I acknowledged with considerable sadness that for my family and me this town represented little more than an historical footnote in a story that began here with the joy brought on by the birth of a child, a joy that gradually gave way to what eventually turned out to be a very different tale.

My father, Mundek Buergenthal, had moved to Lubochna from Germany shortly before Hitler came to power in 1933. Together with a friend, Erich Godal, an anti-Nazi political cartoonist working for a major Berlin daily, they decided to open a small hotel in Lubochna, where Godal owned some property. The political situation in Germany was becoming ever more perilous for Jews and for those who opposed Hitler and the ideology of his National Socialist Party. My father and Godal apparently also believed that the German people's enthusiasm for Hitler would wane in a few years and that they would then be able to return to Berlin. In the meantime, the proximity of Czechoslovakia to Germany would allow them to follow developments back home more closely and enable them to provide temporary refuge to any of their friends who might have to leave Germany in a hurry.

My father was born in 1901 in Galicia, a region of Poland that was part of the Austro-Hungarian Empire before the First

Berlin

Leipzig
Dresden
Podmokly
Liberec
Krkonoše
Moldava
Ústí n. L.
Chomutov
Teplice
Litoměřice
Turnov
Trutnov
C. Lípa
Náchod
Frant. Jáchymov
Lázně
Roudnice
Mělník
Jičín
K. Dvůr
Cheb Karlovy Vary
Žatec
Louny
Ml. Boleslav
K. Hradec
Praha
Mar. Lázně
Rakovník
Poděbrady
Choceň
Stříbro
Beroun
Kolín
Pardubice
Plzeň
Příbram
Benešov
Čáslav
Č. Třebová
Domažlice
Klatovy
Tábor
Pelhřimov
Něm. Brod
Žďár
Sušice
Písek
Blansko
Železn. Ruda
Strakonice
Jindř. Hradec
Jihlava
Regensburg
Vimperk
Prachatice
Třeboň
Budějovice
-Mor.
Brno
Volary
C. Budějovice
Znojmo
C. Krumlov
C. Velenice
Passau
Hor. Dvořiště
Linz
Wien
München
AUTRICHE
Salzburg
Zagreb
Trieste

# HAUS GODAL
## LUBOCHNA · TATRA

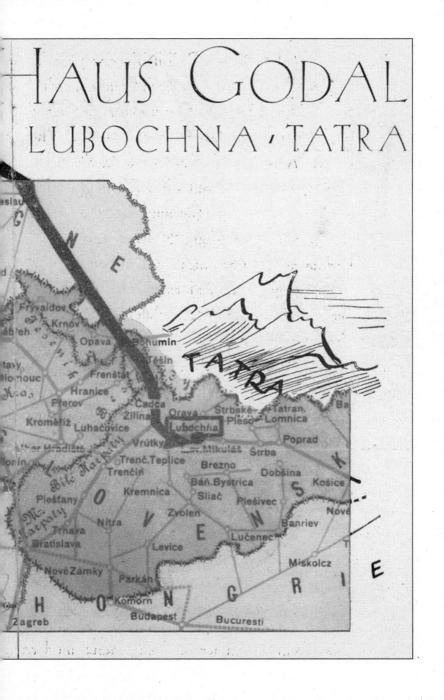

STAATSBAD LUBOCHNA, das slowa
Karlsbad, liegt 600 m hoch traumhaft sch
den dichten Gebirgswäldern der Tatra, um
von einem romantischen Kranz 12–1500 m
Berge. Man erreicht Lubochna in elf
stündiger D=Zug=Faht ab Berlin über
Breslau = Oderberg (Bohumin). Ab
15. Mai ist es D=Zug=Station. Lu=
bochna gehört noch nicht zu den Kur=
orten, in denen sich der lärmende Betrieb
der Großstadt fortsetzt. Alles ist zu

absoluter Erho=
lung geschaffen:
die herrlicheGe=
birgs=Waldluft,
das mildeKlima,
die tiefe Ruhe
des     Gebirgs=
tales.

Zwischen Kur=
haus und Post, völlig zentral liegt das H
GODAL in einem herrlichen 12000 qm g
Garten. Es ist ein Landhaus mit 18 Zim
Alle Fremdenzimmer sind mit ganz mod

sche niedrigen farbigen Lackmöbeln eingerichtet, jedes
n in Zimmer hat fließendes warmes und kaltes Wasser.
-ben — Die Mahlzeiten werden auf der 22 m langen
oher Glasveranda eingenommen, die dem Gebirge zu=

gewandt liegt.—
Der Garten hat
Liegewiesen, für
jeden Gast ist
ein Liegestuhl
vorgesehen.

Besonderer Wert
ist auf die Ver=
pflegung gelegt,
die absolut erst=

klassig ist und nach deutsch=böhmischer Art
zubereitet wird. Der Speisezettel eines Tages
sieht ungefähr so aus:

Frühstück: 2 Eier oder Aufschnitt ‹ Butter,
Konfitüren, Gebäck, Kaffee, Tee oder
Kakao nach Wahl.

AUS Mittag: Suppe od. Pastete, 1 Fleischgang mit Ge=
ßen müse, Früchte od. Kompott, Süßspeise, Mokka.

ern Abends: 1 warmer Fleischgang, Käseplatte oder
nen Früchte.

World War. German and Polish were the languages in which he received his primary and much of his secondary education. His parents lived on a farm that belonged to a wealthy Polish landowner whose extensive estate was administered by my paternal grandfather, an unusual occupation for a Jew at that time in that part of the world. The Polish landowner had been my grandfather's commanding officer in the Austrian army and took him into his service when both returned to civilian life. Eventually he put my grandfather in charge of his many farms.

The nearest school was in a town some distance away. Family lore has it that, to get there, my father was for a time boarded at the home of the flagman in charge of a strategically located level crossing. Trains to and from the town would pass the crossing daily. Since there was no train station nearby, the flagman would slow the train down in the morning and again in the afternoon so that my father might jump on and off. Less hazardous arrangements were later made for him to attend school.

After graduating from high school and a brief stint in the Polish army during the Russo-Polish war which began in 1919, my father enrolled in the law school of the University of Krakow. Before completing his studies, however, he left Poland and moved to Berlin. There he joined his older sister, who was married to a well-known Berlin couturier, and obtained a job with a private Jewish bank. He rose rapidly, becoming an officer of the bank at a relatively young age following his success in helping to manage the bank's investment portfolio. His position at the bank and his brother-in-law's social contacts enabled him to meet many Berlin-based writers, journalists and actors. The rise of Hitler and the ever increasing attacks by his followers on Jews and anti-Nazi intellectuals, quite a number of whom were friends of my father, prompted him to leave Germany and settle in Lubochna.

Gerda Silbergleit, my mother, or Mutti to me, arrived at my father's hotel in 1933. She had travelled from Göttingen, the German university town where she was born and where her parents owned a shoe store. Not quite twenty-one years old at the time – she was born in 1912 – her parents had sent her to Lubochna in the hope that a vacation in Czechoslovakia would help her forget the non-Jewish boyfriend who wanted to marry her. They also thought that it would be good for their daughter to leave Göttingen for a while. There the harassment of Jews – and, in particular, of young Jewish women – by Nazi youths roaming the streets was making life increasingly unpleasant for her.

When making arrangements for my mother's stay at the hotel, her parents asked that she be met at the German border. Instead of sending his driver, my father decided to drive alone to the border, where he gave her the impression that he was the hotel's chauffeur. She was quite embarrassed at dinner to find herself seated at the table of the hotel's owner, the very same driver she had quizzed about Mr Buergenthal, whom her mother had described as a very eligible bachelor. Years later,

*Gerda and Mundek Buergenthal*

whenever I heard my mother tell this story, I wondered whether her visit to Lubochna had been arranged by her parents with a possible marriage to my father in mind, and whether, if there was such a plan, my father knew of it. Was it just a coincidence that his hotel was recommended to my mother's parents by a friend who also knew my father well? I never did find out. To my mother, it was always love at first sight, and that was it!

That may well be true, for my parents were engaged three days after they met, and married a few weeks later, though not before my maternal grandparents, Paul and Rosa Silbergleit (née Blum), had travelled to Lubochna to pass judgement on the prospective bridegroom. They were apparently somewhat taken aback by the rapidity of the engagement and the hasty marriage, but in the Europe of 1933 there was little time for courting. I was born eleven months later. By 1939 we were refugees on the run, only a few steps ahead of the Germans – a whole country, it seemed, had declared war on a family of three whose only crime was that they were Jews.

As I search my memory for some aspects of my brief life in Lubochna, I have a hard time separating what my parents told me from what I actually remember. My guess is that much of what I think I remember from that period I actually heard later from either my father or mother. My mother frequently recalled that I served as her interpreter at the age of three or four when she went shopping in Slovakia. She spoke only German and the shopkeepers for the most part only Slovak. I could apparently get along in both languages. We spoke German at home when all three of us were together, and I must have picked up Slovak from my Slovak nannies.

My only clear recollection of life in Lubochna dates back to a day in late 1938 or early 1939, when my parents told me that we had to leave our hotel. As they began to pack our belongings, they appeared to be very much in a hurry. Years later I was told that the Hlinka Guard, the fascist party that controlled Slovakia with the support of Nazi Germany, claimed to have a court order declaring one of its front organisations the owners of our hotel. (My parents had purchased Erich Godal's share in the hotel some years earlier.) There was no way to challenge this confiscation of our home: by that time, the Hlinka Guard and its followers controlled the courts, and their police threatened to expel us from the country if we resisted their takeover and failed to leave Lubochna immediately.

As a result, we could take only a few suitcases with us, leaving everything else, in addition to the hotel itself, to the new 'owners'. But I wanted my car to come with us! It was a little red car with pedals. I was reassured that we would soon be back and that it would be waiting for me on our return. That car was my most treasured possession. I must have sensed that I would never see it again, for I went to the storeroom to say goodbye to it. There it was, propped up on its rear wheels, leaning against a post, surrounded by boxes and suitcases. It looked as sad as I felt. To this day, when I think back to that moment, I can still see my little red car.

*Thomas with his parents, May 1937*

After leaving Lubochna we lived for a time in Zilina, also in Slovakia. At first we stayed with friends who owned the Grand Hotel there. I remember the name because I had a wonderful time standing at its main entrance with one of the doormen and, as was then the custom, calling out 'Grand Hotel!' to passers-by. They would frequently engage me in conversation and, to my delight, sometimes even toss me a coin.

From the hotel we moved to a small apartment. Here my mother and I were often alone. My father had found a job as a travelling salesman for a medical-instrument company and spent a lot of time visiting customers in different parts of the country. My parents had apparently used most of their savings, including the money my mother had received from her parents as dowry, to enlarge the hotel and to buy out their former part-ner. Now the hotel was gone and with it the income they had depended on.

While we lived in Lubochna, Mutti had never had to cook. That was done by the hotel's chef, a massive and intimidating Slovak matron, who let my father know in no uncertain terms that his young wife was not welcome in her kitchen. Now, in Zilina, things were different and I soon realised that my mother was not a very good cook. Once she roasted a chicken without gutting it properly and my father ended up with a mouthful of corn, which must have been the remains of the chicken's last meal. Of course, he spat it all out and they had a big fight. 'I thought they taught you something at that finishing school in Göttingen!' screamed my father. Mutti counter-attacked by

*The red car – Thomas's favourite toy, 1937*

reminding him of some long-forgotten incident for which he was supposedly to blame. And when he replied that that had nothing to do with her inability to cook, she accused him of changing the subject. I soon understood that she would always win these arguments, while he would end up shaking his head in disbelief. At times she would make me her co-conspirator. Once, when she discovered that the kitchen rag she had been looking for had fallen into the pot with our evening meal, she swore me to secrecy and assured me that 'Papa will not notice anything if we don't tell.'

One day, while my father was out of town, the police came to our apartment and ordered my mother to pack our belongings and make sure that we would be ready to go with them within the hour. We were Jews and undesirable foreigners, we were told, and were being expelled from the country. My mother protested that we could not leave without my father, but to no avail. We were taken to the police station. Its building and courtyard were already filled with other foreigners. My mother recognised some of our friends among them. People were sitting on their suitcases, children were crying, and I sensed that everybody was very afraid, just as I was.

As soon as we arrived at the police station my mother, in her precise, clipped German, demanded to see the person in charge. She made a tremendous amount of noise while waving a leather-bound document with a lot of stamps on it. After a few minutes we were taken into an office. Here a heavyset man in uniform, who was not very friendly, asked in a threatening

The Buergenthal family, already on the run, Slovakia, circa 1938

tone of voice what all the commotion was about and who she thought she was. My mother, who seemed very tall to me at that moment, but who measured slightly less than five feet, slammed her document on the man's desk and barked at him in German, 'We are Germans!' Pointing to the document on the desk, which she told him was her passport, she continued in that same tone, 'We are supposed to be your allies! It is an outrage that you are treating us like common criminals.' She wanted to be taken to the German consul immediately to protest this scandalous treatment, and she warned the police official that he and his superiors were going to be in very serious trouble with the German authorities for molesting Germans living peacefully in Slovakia. 'Just you wait and see what will happen when my husband comes back and does not find us at home!'

After a whispered conversation with another man and some further inspection of the passport, the officer suddenly smiled at us, got up from behind his desk, grasped my mother's hand and, in broken German, apologised to her profusely. This was all a big mistake; of course they were not deporting Germans living in Slovakia, only foreign Jews and other undesirables who should not have been allowed into the country in the first place. He shook my mother's hand again, saluted and ordered a policeman to escort us home.

Years later I learned that my mother's 'passport' was in fact a German driving licence. Her German passport had been confiscated when she tried to renew it because, like other Jews living abroad, she had apparently been stripped of her German nationality. To this day I wonder what she would have done had the police officer been able to read German and called her bluff. The last person she wanted to talk to at that moment was the German consul.

I continue to marvel at the courage, ingenuity and intelligence my mother demonstrated that day, character traits she was to reveal many times over in the future in even more difficult circumstances. Where did this young woman from a well-to-do, protective Jewish middle-class home with barely a secondary-school education derive the cunning and almost reckless gall to assess and take advantage of the weakness of those posing a serious threat to her or her family, and come out the winner? As a child I assumed that it was only natural for my mother to always know what to do. But what was then 'natural' has continued over the years to inspire my profound admiration and to puzzle me, not only because she repeatedly succeeded in beating the odds when confronting the Nazi killing machine, but because she seemed to pull off these successes at a moment's notice with the speed of a magician. Where did that magic come from? Although I have tried, I have never quite been able to pin down the intellectual and emotional source of my mother's special gift. All I know is that she had it.

As soon as we had returned to our apartment from the police station Mutti exclaimed, 'We were lucky this time!' But then she added, 'They will be back,' and began to look for my father's handgun. He had acquired it in Lubochna to scare off foxes or other animals that sometimes tried to get into the chicken coop behind the hotel's woodshed. When my mother found the gun, she told me that we had to throw it away secretly so that the police would not find it the next time they came. She handled the gun very gingerly, let it slide into a paper bag and told me not to touch it. The next day we walked to the river and threw the gun into the water from one of the bridges. I did not understand it, but felt very grown up to be participating in this highly secret operation. When my father returned he was very angry to learn that my mother had thrown his gun away, but it was too late to do anything about it.

A few days later my parents decided that Slovakia was no longer safe for us and that the time had come to leave. They expected the harassment of Jews, particularly foreign Jews, to become more severe in that part of Czechoslovakia. My father was also afraid that he might be on a Gestapo 'Wanted' list, and that if the police were to come back, they might arrest him and turn him over to the Germans. But where could we go? That was a question I heard my parents discuss over and over again in whispered tones, usually at night when I was supposed to be asleep. Eventually they settled on Poland. It was the only country, they thought, that might let us enter. There, moreover, my father would be able to obtain the visas that he had been promised by the British authorities in Czechoslovakia and that would allow us to travel to England as political refugees.

Soon we were on our way. Getting to Poland and getting into Poland, however, were two entirely different matters. We became trapped in the no-man's-land between Poland and Czechoslovakia. This strip of land measured some fifty yards from border to border. The border posts were connected by a dirt road that cut through a field. On either side of the road ran a deep drainage ditch. At the Polish side of the border, the guards refused us entry and ordered us back to the Czech side, but the Czechs would not allow us to re-enter and ordered us to leave. And so it went for days. That strip of road seemed to grow longer and longer on each of the many occasions we were forced to tramp from one end to the other, carrying or pushing our suitcases while the border guards kept yelling at us not to show up again.

We must have been stateless and had no valid travel documents. My father probably lost his Polish nationality under a Polish law, enacted in 1938, which stripped Polish citizens of their nationality if they had remained outside of Poland for more than five years. I do not know whether he had earlier acquired German nationality, but if he had, he would have lost it, as did my mother, when the Nazis denaturalised Jews living abroad. Stateless, we had no right either to enter Poland or to return to Czechoslovakia. Every day and every night my father would wait for a new shift of guards on the Polish side of the border. As soon as they arrived he would march us up to the guardhouse and ask to be admitted, claiming that he was a Pole. But since he lacked the necessary papers to prove it, the guards would order us to return to the Czech side. Back and forth we went, day and night. We would sleep in the field adjacent to the road or in one of the ditches alongside it. On rare occasions we would be allowed to sleep in the waiting room of one of the guardhouses. While we were cold most of the time, we were not hungry because the Czech or Polish farmers would sell us bread and sausages. But we were not going very far. I was tired and did not understand why nobody wanted to let us into their country.

A week or so after we had arrived at the border, on a day when we had been refused entry by the Poles for the umpteenth time, we were met by heavily armed German soldiers on the Czech side. It seems that during our time in no-man's-land Germany had occupied Czechoslovakia, so here we were, in the clutches of the very people from whom we were trying to escape. I could sense that my parents were very afraid. The German who appeared to be in charge wanted to know who we were and what we were doing in the middle of nowhere. My father, who suddenly spoke very poor German, answered that we were Poles, that we had been here for more than a week, and that the Poles would not allow us to return to our own country. 'We shall see about that,' snarled the German officer. With those words he ordered two of his soldiers to come over and pick up our suitcases. I thought that they were going to do something terrible to us, because my mother suddenly grasped my hand very tightly and stopped me from speaking. But the German soldiers merely led us back to the Polish border. Once there, they ordered the Polish guards to let us pass. 'These people are Poles!' yelled one the soldiers. 'I order you to let them in. You had better not send them to our side again. Things are going to be different from now on!' My father translated what the German was saying and the Poles nodded obediently.

That is how we got into Poland. It must have been March 1939, for that is when Germany marched into Czechoslovakia. I was almost five years old.

*Chapter 2*

# Katowice

I have no recollection of our first days in Poland. We must have stayed in a boarding house or rented room for a short while, and I probably slept through most of it. My first memory is of the three of us sitting on a horse-drawn hay wagon with our suitcases piled up at one end. The driver was an old man with a long white beard. He wore a black hat and spoke with my father in a language that sounded German, but which I could barely understand. These were the first Yiddish words I had ever heard and he was the first Chasidic Jew I had ever seen. I can still recall hearing the driver say something about a *Schuh*, the German for shoe, and wondering why our footwear was important. Only much later, when I picked up Yiddish from my playmates in the ghetto of Kielce, did I learn that a *shoo* meant an hour in Yiddish, and that the driver had told my father that it would take about an hour for us to reach our destination.

Our next stop was Warsaw. Here my father had relatives, and since neither my mother nor I had ever met any of them we were greeted with much rejoicing and kissing, lots of laughter and enormous amounts of food everywhere we went. I hated these visits because all the women kept kissing me and stuffing me with food. Fortunately there were always some children around with whom I could escape from the grown-ups and play.

These visits came to an end after I caught a severe case of whooping cough from one of my playmates. The doctor told my parents that inhaling river air would work wonders for me. To my delight, my parents acted almost immediately on the doctor's recommendation and hired a horse-drawn carriage to drive me back and forth across a bridge over the Vistula that connected Warsaw with Praga, its eastern suburb. I loved these daily excursions, and was very sad when my cough gradually subsided and my parents decided that we could now leave Warsaw and travel to Katowice.

By 1939 Katowice, a city in the southern part of Poland, had become a gathering point for German Jewish refugees. Here they registered with the British consulate in the hope of obtaining the necessary documents allowing them to travel to England. My parents had been told in Warsaw that the British consulate in Katowice would handle our visa applications, and that the sooner we got there the sooner we would be able to leave for England. My whooping cough had delayed our departure.

In Katowice we moved into a small apartment. I'll never forget our first night there. My parents had barely turned off the lights when the room we all shared seemed to come alive. My mother screamed that she was being bitten to death. When my father jumped out of bed and switched on the light we saw that the walls and our beds were covered with bedbugs. They were crawling all over us. It was quite a sight to behold: there seemed to be hundreds of ugly orange-yellow bugs with a vicious bite that itched intolerably.

My mother wanted to leave right away, but my father calmed her down and explained to her that we were lucky to have this place. Once they had convinced themselves that we had no choice but to stay, my parents mounted a veritable bedbug extermination campaign. They found some candles and began to burn the bugs off the walls; they shook them out of the sheets and stepped on them on the floor. There was a sink in the room and my mother started shaking the insects from the sheets into the sink in the hope of drowning them. These desperate efforts to rid us of vermin must have gone on all night, though I fell asleep after a while. Little did I know that bedbugs would be the least of our problems in the years that lay ahead.

I had a lot of fun in Katowice. There the refugees formed their own little community. My parents became part of it and soon made many friends in this group. As was customary in Germany, these friends immediately became my 'uncles' and 'aunts'. I played with their children, and they kept an eye on me when my parents were unable to. They usually gathered in a café or park. Here they played cards, read newspapers, whispered a lot about the war that was coming, and worried.

Everybody was waiting for their 'lucky day'. And every so often there would be a celebration, much kissing, many tears: somebody's lucky day had arrived in the form of a long-awaited visa from the British consulate, allowing the recipient to travel to England. Soon those who had been granted visas would leave Katowice, usually in small groups or transports put together by the British.

Our lucky day was not to come for some time. In the meantime, I remember playing in a lovely park in Katowice and swimming in a nearby lake. The Jewish community of the city apparently provided some help for needy refugees, as did various individuals associated with it. I remember one day being taken shopping by a very nice man who had befriended my parents, and returning home with toys and wearing a completely new outfit: new trousers, shirt and jacket. He had thought I looked too German in the clothes my mother liked me to wear. From time to time we would also be invited to dinner in Jewish homes, although this did not happen all that often, and certainly not as often as I would have liked; I would have been happy to escape our ugly room and meagre meals.

One day my mother came home in a very excited state. She told my father that she and a girlfriend had gone to a famous fortune-teller. Before going in, she had taken off her wedding ring and, because she looked much younger than her age – she was twenty-seven at the time – she was very surprised when the fortune-teller, after studying her cards, proclaimed that my mother was married and had one child. Besides knowing a great deal about our family background, the fortune-teller told my mother that her son was *ein Glückskind* – a lucky child – and that he would emerge unscathed from the future that awaited us.

My father scolded my mother for believing this nonsense and spending money on it when we had barely any left. But my mother claimed that her girlfriend paid for the visit because she wanted someone to accompany her. 'Besides, maybe the fortune-teller knows something we don't, for how else could she have known so much about me?' she retorted. 'The only thing the fortune-teller knows that we don't know is how to make money in these bad times,' barked my father. The argument between them continued for a while.

None of us could have known at the time, and I only found out much later, that the fortune-teller's prediction about me would serve to sustain my mother's hopes in the years to come, when we were separated. Even after the war, when friends tried to convince her to give up the search for me and not to continue torturing herself, for 'Tommy could not possibly have survived,' she would reply that she knew that I was alive. To me she insisted years later that everything the fortune-teller had told her had come true. 'Of course, I don't believe in this hocus-pocus,' she would add in all earnestness, only to contradict herself immediately by asking, 'But how do you explain that she was right about you and me?'

Our lucky day came a few weeks after my mother's visit to the fortune-teller. We received the prized visas for travel to

England and were scheduled to leave Katowice on 1 September 1939. There was the usual excitement among our friends, with everybody wishing us well and expressing the hope that we would all soon be reunited in England. I was told that we would be in England in a few weeks and that, once there, we would no longer have to be afraid of the Nazis.

But it was not to be: on our 'lucky day' Hitler decided to invade Poland. When we arrived at Katowice station, where our transport was to be assembled, the British officials told us that it was no longer possible to leave from a Polish port. Arrangements had therefore been made to get us to England via the Balkans. Despite the onrush of people who were trying to leave Katowice that morning, probably because it was not far from the German border, we eventually got to board the carriage reserved for us and some other refugees who had also received their visas. Finally, after a long delay, the train moved out of the station. We seemed to have made it.

I don't know how long we travelled on that train. For the most part, though, the train was standing more than moving, waiting for other trains, loaded with soldiers, to pass. The roads alongside the railroad line were crowded with people walking or riding in horse-drawn carriages and wagons. Everywhere there were long Polish army columns, marching, on horseback or on trucks, pulling artillery pieces and supplies. The soldiers were moving in the opposite direction from the civilians, who had to make room for them to pass on the narrow roads.

For me, all this commotion was very exciting. I spent much time waving to the passing soldiers and admiring their three-cornered hats and uniforms. And then, suddenly, the fun stopped. Our train had again halted, this time next to a train filled with Polish soldiers and military equipment. On either side of the tracks were open fields. We had probably not been standing there for more than a few minutes when we began to hear the far-off sounds of approaching aeroplanes. Then they were above us – two or three of them. People began to scream, 'Niemcy! Niemcy!' ('Germans! Germans!'), and suddenly the air resounded with the rattle of machine-gun fire and the thump of exploding bombs. The train began to shake. The noise was terrible.

My father grabbed my mother and me and pushed us out of the train. 'They are attacking the military train!' he screamed above the noise. 'We must get out, we must get out.' Some people had already jumped from the train and were scrambling across the tracks into the fields. We followed behind, pushed on by others. The Polish soldiers began to shoot at the German planes with rifles held out of their carriage windows. They did not have much luck. The planes kept swooping down on the trains and the tracks, blowing up some of the carriages. They kept repeating this manoeuvre for what seemed like a very long time.

We managed to reach the nearby field, where my mother threw herself on top of me while my father shielded both of us with his body. People were screaming as the planes flew over us with their machine guns blazing. They could easily have killed all of us, but it seemed we were not their target. Then, just as suddenly as they had appeared, the planes were gone. We waited for a while for them to return and, when they did not, we got up and started to look around. No one on our side of the field seemed to have been hit, but people were wailing and a few children were crying. Some railroad cars were on fire; there was smoke everywhere. Many injured and dead soldiers were lying on the other side of the tracks and near their train. The tracks had been destroyed as far as the eye could see.

After a while my father went to look for our belongings. He found some bags and dragged them back to the field. Here we were soon joined by others from our group. 'What now?' was the question being asked, and 'Where are we?' Nobody seemed to have any answers and, except for my father, no one in the group spoke Polish. He soon learned from some passing farmers that we were not far from Sandomierz, a town about 200 kilometres east of Katowice.

We stayed overnight in a barn and then our little group began the trek east to the Russian border, sometimes in hired horse-drawn wagons and other times on foot. The roads were teeming with civilians and soldiers. Like us, most of the civilians were trying to get away from the invading Germans. Every day there were more people on the road. We slept in open fields or in barns and made little progress in our move east. The farmers would charge us for the use of their barns and sell us food. Often, the barns would already be rented out by the time we arrived, and then we would have to sleep outside. Some farmers were kind to us, others were not. The latter frequently called us bad names. Here I first learned that we were *Parszywe Zydzi* – Scabby Jews.

There were rumours that German spies were everywhere. My father heard that the public was being warned by the Polish government to be on the lookout for 'a German fifth column'. Our little group was suspect because, except for my father, its members spoke only German. With increasing frequency my father would have to explain who we were and show our English travel documents to suspicious Polish officials. After a while, only he would go out to the villages to buy food for our group and to get the latest news. I would sometimes accompany him. There we would listen to a radio or talk to the farmers. The information we would bring back seemed always to be the same: 'Things don't look too good. The Germans are advancing; the Polish army is retreating.'

Every so often my father would speak with somebody who had recently come back from Russia or had news from there. Here, too, the story was usually the same. 'Terrible things are happening in that country. Not a good place for foreigners; many of them are being sent to Siberia.' Nobody in our group wanted to believe these reports since we had hoped to escape to Russia. Finally, my father decided to see for himself. He was back a few days later and announced that it would be better to take our chances in Poland. I don't know whether he had actually crossed into Russia – we were not very far from the border – or whether he had spoken to people who knew, but he was convinced that it would be a mistake for us to try to get into Russia. 'Conditions are terrible,' he reported, 'particularly for foreigners. A lot of people are getting arrested or deported. The lucky ones are turned back at the border.' 'If not Russia, then what?' somebody asked, and there followed a long and often heated discussion about the fate that awaited us in a Poland under German occupation. It continued into the night. When I woke up the next morning, the decision had been made. Instead of seeking to enter Russia, we would try to reach Kielce, a city west of Sandomierz with a large Jewish community that might take us in.

Little had changed on the roads. They were ever more congested. We were being stopped often and asked to produce our papers. At times there were tense moments, with my father trying to convince Polish military officers that we were not German spies. The news from the front was not very good, my father reported. It was getting worse every day. The Poles were blaming German spies for their military setbacks and the rapid German advances.

My father tried to cheer everybody up by telling us that we would soon be in Kielce and sleep in real beds again. That was great news for me, but it had little effect on the grim mood that had gripped our little group. I heard someone say that we did not have much to look forward to. 'We will be shot either by the Poles as spies or by the Nazis because we are Jews.' 'What is better?' one of my 'uncles' asked with a grin, and everybody laughed. After a while, though, nothing seemed to be funny any more.

A few days after our decision to walk to Kielce, we began to hear what sounded like a distant thunderstorm. 'Artillery fire,' my father told me, 'but it is far away from here. Listen,' and he showed me how, by lying down and pressing my ear to the ground, I would be able to hear it much better. I had a lot of fun playing this game. More and more Polish soldiers and their equipment could be seen on the road and in nearby fields. After a while the entire road was taken up by retreating troops, at which point all civilians were ordered off the roads. We waited and rested in a nearby ditch. It seemed to be hours before the last of the Polish soldiers had passed. Then, suddenly, we heard the roar of approaching engines and saw walls of dust in the distance. 'Tanks! German tanks!' I could almost touch the fear that swept over our little group. But then I heard my father's reassuring voice, 'Stay calm! Don't anybody run! Don't say anything unless spoken to.'

As the tanks approached – they advanced towards us on the road and across the fields – we were enveloped in dust and smoke. One of the tanks stopped near our group and a young soldier, his body protruding from the open turret, his face covered in soot, yelled over to us in German, wanting to know who we were. After some hesitation, somebody answered that we were Jews, and another added, 'German Jews'. 'Nothing to worry about,' he yelled back. 'The war will be over soon, and we'll all be able to go home again.' He waved and the tank moved forward. These very reassuring words brought temporary relief to our group. People began to joke and laugh again. But as fate would have it, they turned out to be the kindest words any German would address to us for a long time to come.

Notwithstanding what the young soldier had said, for us the war had really only just begun. We continued towards Kielce. Near Opatów, some sixty kilometres from Kielce, a wealthy Polish farmer allowed us to stay in one of his barns. He and my father would go off to talk for hours at a time. My mother would always worry until my father returned, and the two of them would whisper a lot. Later I learned that the farmer and some of his friends were in the process of forming a Polish resistance group to fight the Germans. They wanted my father to join them; they needed people who spoke German and Polish and had military experience. We would not have to worry about a place to stay or food, and a way would be found to get us false identity papers. My father and mother talked about this offer for days. Eventually, he turned it down. They were both very sad that they had to make this decision. The problem was that although my father and I, because of our features and colouring, could have passed for Poles, my mother spoke no Polish and her wavy dark hair and brown eyes would give her away as Jewish. 'Poles can smell a Jew a mile away,' my father said, 'and sooner or later somebody will denounce us to the Germans.' Together, we could not pass ourselves off as

Poles and expect to get away with it for long, and breaking up the family was out of the question. We continued our trek to Kielce.

It seemed that we were condemned to be who we were, which was not a particularly good prospect. We could do little more than hope that things would get better. That hope never left us, and it sustained us in the years to come, despite the fact that we had no good reason to expect our situation to improve. But what else could we do but hope? That, after all, is human nature.

# Chapter 3

# The Ghetto of Kielce

We lived in Kielce for about four years until we were transported to Auschwitz in early August 1944. 'Lived' is probably not the right word to describe our incarceration in that bleak Polish industrial city, its ghetto and two different work camps. Had our train not been bombed in an area where Kielce was the nearest Polish city with a large Jewish population – it numbered about 25,000 at the time – we would not have gone there, although, in retrospect, it made little difference that we did not reach another Polish city. The fate of Jews was basically the same in all of them, and life in Kielce during those years was no worse or better than elsewhere in Poland.

My first recollection of Kielce is our one-room (kitchen included) apartment on the third floor of an old crumbling apartment house on Silniczna Street, part of a four-building complex that surrounded a dirty courtyard. From the courtyard a large entrance gate opened on to a noisy street. We were assigned the apartment by the Jewish community council of the city shortly before the ghetto was established in early 1940. At that time the German police (the Schutzpolizei) and the Gestapo ordered all Jews to move into the area of the city containing the largest concentration of its Jewish population, which was also one of the most run-down parts of town. We did not have to move; we were there already.

Until my father got a job as a cook's helper in the Schutzpolizei kitchen outside the ghetto, we had very little to eat. During those early days food could still be bought from the outside. The more prosperous Jewish families lived relatively well compared with us, since we had hardly any money even after my mother sold almost all her jewellery. In his new job, my father would return home every evening with a large canteen of food. He usually hid pieces of meat under the mashed potatoes and vegetables he was allowed to take with him. By mid-afternoon my mother and I would already be waiting for him and our one good meal of the day. From time to time we were invited by wealthy families in the neighbourhood to join them for a Sabbath meal. I remember looking forward to these dinners because of the food. But I also dreaded them because they were always preceded by what seemed to me interminably long prayers.

Soon I found another way to get some food, and on rare occasions even a little money. Because religious Jews are not allowed to work on the Sabbath or on Jewish holidays, they may not perform most household chores on those days, including lighting ovens and fireplaces or turning on lights in their homes. These chores had in the past been performed by non-Jewish servants or Poles hired for the purpose. After non-Jews were barred from entering the ghetto, I was asked by some of our neighbours, who knew that we were not observant Jews, to perform these functions. That is how I became a *Shabbat goy*, a Sabbath gentile. I liked doing these chores, not only because I was paid for them, but also because I got to know many families in the neighbourhood and was able to see how they lived and what their homes looked like. I was fascinated by the appearance of the very orthodox Jews – their long *payess* (sideburn-locks), their *tzitzit* (cloth fringes), their black hats and caftans, as well as the *talaysim* (prayer shawls) and the *tefillin* (phylacteries) they wore on their arms and foreheads when praying. But the majority of the people in the ghetto were not orthodox and dressed just as we did.

Once all Jews had been moved into what became the Ghetto of Kielce, the area was surrounded by walls and fences, guarded by Jewish and Polish police as well as the Schutzpolizei. There were many children in our neighbourhood and I soon had lots of friends. In those early days, some Poles were still allowed to come in, mostly to sell vegetables and milk. When winter came, Polish farmers would enter the ghetto with their horse-drawn wagons to sell firewood, which was very expensive. We kids would wait for them and jump on the back of the wagons, hoping that the driver would not see us before we had a chance to grab some of the wood and run off with it. If he saw us, he would try to slash at us with his long whip. Sometimes he would succeed, despite the avoiding techniques we developed over time. Besides needing the wood, we had a lot of fun playing this game, particularly since our parents, while not approving of our wagon-jumping, were always pleased to get the few pieces of wood we brought in.

Another game I remember playing with my friends was hiding near the open ground behind our apartment complex. Peasant women would sometimes urinate there in a standing position with their legs spread out, but without lifting their long skirts. At some point mid-stream we would whistle or bang on a can in the hope of startling them and making them move – with the predictable result. We would then run away laughing, while the women would hurl terrible Polish curses at us.

Once two of my friends and I found a leather box of tefillin used by religious Jews in their prayers. Somebody had told us never to open such a box, that it was a sin to do so, and that God would strike down anyone who took out the little piece of parchment it contained, with its Hebrew inscription from the Torah. But we had also heard that if you found that piece of parchment and put it under your armpit, you would be able to fly. Well, we had quite a dilemma on our hands: we wanted to be able to fly, but were afraid of God's wrath. Eventually, and with trembling hands, we cut open the box, expecting lightning to strike us right there and then, but nothing happened. One of the older boys very cautiously placed the parchment under his arm and readied himself for take-off. Again nothing happened. Then, one after the other, we each tried the same manoeuvre with equal lack of success. Disappointed, but still afraid of God's punishment, we threw the box away and promised not to tell anyone what we had done.

In Poland, the expression *Yekke*, a somewhat derogatory term of ridicule, was applied by Polish Jews to German Jews, who generally spoke no Yiddish or Polish and who, because of their appearance or demeanour, were thought by many Polish Jews to look more like gentiles and to be naive in matters of business. To Polish Jews my mother was a *Yekkete* (a female *Yekke*) and when she and I walked through certain neighbourhoods, we were frequently called 'Yekkes!' by the local children. Once, while walking alone, I found myself surrounded by a group of boys my age and older. They began to push me around, making fun of my clothes and calling me 'Yekke putz, Yekke putz', the latter being a bad word I had been told never to use. I managed to run away but swore vengeance. My opportunity arrived soon when, a few days later, I saw a boy walking with his mother on our street and recognised him as one of my tormentors. I raced up behind him, gave him a push with all my might and ran away. He fell and cut his lip. When his mother saw the blood she began to scream and wail, hurling vile Yiddish and Polish curses at me, my family and my descendants. I could hear her from the far side of our courtyard where I was hiding. My mother was very mad at me when she heard what I had done, and told my father. I expected to receive a severe spanking, but after hearing the whole story he said that it was good that I was learning to defend myself and, while he did not approve of my attack from behind, it was too late to do much about it.

Soon life in the ghetto became increasingly difficult and dangerous, and our games began to give way to fear that kept us off the streets. There was one German – either from the Gestapo or the Schutzpolizei – who would walk through the ghetto killing people at random. He would walk up behind them, shoot them in the back of the neck and move on. News that he was around would spread like wildfire and in no time at all the streets were deserted. I once saw him from a distance and ran home as fast as I could. After that I was afraid to play in the street and no longer thought that our courtyard was safe.

As time went on the Germans would conduct so-called *razzias* or raids with ever greater frequency. As a rule, a raid would begin with a contingent of heavily armed soldiers driving up to a house. They would storm inside, pull people out and drag them into their trucks. Anyone who resisted was kicked and beaten. Sometimes people were shot on the spot. Once, when I heard a lot of noise in our courtyard, I ran to the window and saw Germans pouring into the building across from ours. Minutes later I heard terrible screams coming from one of the apartments there. It served as a *chaydar* (religious school) as well as the living quarters of the rabbi who instructed a few children in violation of the German prohibition against teaching. The rabbi's wife and grown daughters were made to undress and stand naked in the courtyard while the rabbi, his hat knocked off his head, was dragged out of the house by his beard and taken away.

At other times the Gestapo or the Schutzpolizei would drive into the ghetto, randomly grab men with beards and order them to cut off each other's beards and side-locks. Those who resisted were severely beaten. The soldiers seemed to be enjoying themselves. They would laugh a lot and make fun of their victims, who were shaking with fear and pleaded to be allowed to keep their beards. Jews also had to doff their hats when encountering a German soldier on the street. If a Jew did not do so, the Germans would knock his hat off and beat him. But if he did, they would frequently also beat him, yelling, 'Why are you greeting me, you dirty Jew? I am not your friend!' My father avoided this problem by never wearing a hat, not even on the coldest days of those terrible Polish winters. 'Why give them the pleasure?' he would say when people called him a *meshoogene* (crazy man) for not wearing a hat.

Every so often we would hear that this or that community leader or some other person had been picked up by the Gestapo, never to reappear. My father and mother would discuss these events in whispered tones. Then I would hear one of them say that the victims must have been denounced to the Gestapo by our own people, and that one had to be very careful what one said and to whom. 'The walls have ears,' one of them would invariably say, and while I did not quite understand what that expression meant, I soon learned not to tell anyone what I heard in our apartment or those of our neighbours, where my father and mother and their friends would gather in the evenings to talk and occasionally share some vodka that someone had been able to find.

Not long after the ghetto was established, the Jewish community council put my father in charge of the office that allocated living quarters to the many people who had been moved there. He did not really want that job, since it put an end to the food he brought home from the police kitchen, but he felt that he could not decline. The previous housing manager had been dismissed following allegations of corruption. Not long after he took this job, I remember my father throwing two men out of our apartment. He was very angry, and I later heard him tell my mother that the men had offered a large bribe in return for a bigger apartment. That prompted my mother to ask why he did not get us a bigger apartment now that he had that power. My father just looked at her, shaking his head in disbelief. We continued to live in the same little place first assigned to us when we arrived in Kielce.

After bringing some order to the ghetto housing office, my father was put in charge of the *Werkstatt*, or workshop, which resembled a small factory. Here tailors, shoemakers, furriers, hatters and other artisans had to work for the Gestapo and Schutzpolizei, performing whatever tasks they were ordered to do. For the most part they made clothes and shoes for the officers and their wives. The *Werkstatt* was just outside the ghetto walls, which meant that my father and all those who worked there had permits to get to their workplace.

Not long after my father became the head of the *Werkstatt*, my parents found out that my maternal grandparents had been deported from their home in Göttingen to the Ghetto of Warsaw. How they got that news I do not know, but I remember my parents talking day and night about my grandparents and what could be done to bring them to Kielce. I heard my father say, 'I'll talk to one of the officers of the Schutzpolizei. His wife has a big appetite for the fur coats we have been making for her; he also seems to be more human than the others.' Not long afterwards, my grandparents arrived in Kielce. To me it was a miracle, the nicest thing that had happened to us in years. My mother was very, very happy, and I finally had grandparents like some of my friends!

My grandparents were provided with a room not far from where we lived. I would visit them daily and hear wonderful stories about my mother when she was a young girl, about her brother Eric who lived in America, and about their life in Göttingen before the Nazis came. They had seen me a few times when I was just a baby, but as far as I was concerned, this was my first meeting with them. Visiting them was like entering another world, a world far removed from the ghetto, one full of love and tranquillity. Here I felt safe and protected. The stories they told me about the past and the future transported me to a place where all people lived in peace and where being a Jew was not a crime.

The two families we were closest to in our apartment house were the Friedmanns and the Lachses. They were related to

*Rosa Blum-Silbergleit, Thomas's grandmother*

each other and still lived in their pre-war apartments, one floor below us. My father and mother would often be guests in their homes, and I would play there with their children, Ucek and Zarenka, who were cousins. Zarenka was about four years old; Ucek must have been a year or so older. When I asked why the Friedmanns and the Lachses always had good food, I was told that they were rich and that when the war was over, we too would be rich again and have all the food we could eat. It was not easy for me to understand why we had to wait for the end of the war to be rich, but I kept these thoughts to myself.

One morning in August 1942, while it was still very dark, we were awakened by loud honking, repeated bursts of gunfire and announcements over loudspeakers: '*Alle raus, alle raus! Wer nicht raus kommt wird erschossen!*' ('All out, all out! Anyone who does not come out will be shot!') The ghetto was being

Paul Silbergleit, Thomas's grandfather

liquidated or, in the words bellowing out of the loudspeakers, 'Aussiedlung! Aussiedlung!' ('Evacuation!') People were scream-ing and crying all around us. My mother immediately began to pack some of our belongings, while pleading with my father to hurry up. He was standing over our kitchen sink, shaving very deliberately and telling my mother to be quiet. 'Let me think!' I heard him repeat over and over again. It was all very eerie, and the noise outside was getting louder and louder. When my father finished shaving he put away his straight razor, helped my mother pack a few more things and told us to follow him. There was shooting all around us, with one or two gunshots at a time coming from some of the houses the Germans had begun to search. When they encountered sick or old people who could not leave, they would simply shoot them on the spot and move on. We were the last family to come out of our build-ing, just ahead of the marauding German death squads.

Our courtyard was crowded with our neighbours, who were trying to get away from the soldiers with their incessantly bark-ing dogs that seemed to be trained to attack when their han-dlers yelled 'Jude!' My father pushed through the crowd, trying to lead us out of the courtyard with his Werkstatt pass in hand. Whenever he recognised one of his workers, he would urge them and their families to follow him. Gradually, some twenty to thirty people joined our group.

Along the way we searched for my grandparents, but they were nowhere to be found. I never saw them again. To this day, I can still picture them, their smiles when I entered their little apartment, and the feeling of peace and happiness their embraces and kisses brought me.

As my father led us towards the ghetto wall and the entrance to the *Werkstatt* we were stopped again and again by heavily armed soldiers, who would yell and point their guns at us in a most threatening manner. That was very scary. There was still a lot of shooting all around us, bodies were lying in the streets and we could not be sure that the German patrols we encountered would not shoot us as well. As soon as we were stopped my father would inform the soldiers, in roughly the same tone of voice as they used when addressing us, that he was under strict orders by the commandant of the city to protect the *Werkstatt*. We would then be allowed to continue. 'Never show them that you are afraid of them,' I remember my father telling me time and again.

When we reached our destination my father locked the gate and told everyone to settle down for the day. The shooting continued all around us for much of the afternoon. After a while some men in our group pleaded with my father to let us march out 'before they come in and kill us all for disobeying orders'. My father would have none of it and insisted repeatedly that our chances of survival were much greater if we remained in the *Werkstatt* until things had calmed down in the ghetto.

We stayed in the *Werkstatt* for a few more hours. Had we wanted to, we could have escaped from there into the Polish part of the city, but without false papers and a lot of money we would soon have been caught and most likely executed. So we remained in the *Werkstatt* until the shooting had died down. At that point my father decided that the time had come for us to move out. Once again we were stopped repeatedly by German patrols. My father would inform them that he was under orders to bring the workers of the *Werkstatt* to the officer in charge of the evacuation. We would then be allowed to continue on our way to a large square.

Along the way, we passed a group of German soldiers. They had surrounded two young Poles who were on their knees, pleading for their lives. Next to them were two sacks with part of their contents strewn around. One of the Poles was wearing the whitest shoes I had ever seen. The soldiers were kicking the young men and yelling that looting was punishable by death. Then they shot them. For years afterwards, whenever I saw or heard that someone had been shot, the image of the young man on his knees with those white shoes would invariably revive memories of that terrible scene.

As we approached the square we could see a group of Gestapo and Schutzpolizei officers facing a large crowd of ghetto inmates, all pleading to be allowed to cross over to the other side of the yard, where the people who had been selected to remain in Kielce after the liquidation of the ghetto were standing. As we entered the yard, with my father in the lead, the commandant of the Schutzpolizei, who was a frequent customer at the *Werkstatt*, recognised him. 'We need him,' he exclaimed, 'he runs the *Werkstatt*!' and he motioned my father to the other side. My mother, holding on to me, followed.

When a soldier tried to stop us, the officer motioned him to let us through. Once we were together, my father pointed to the group he had led out of the *Werkstatt* and told an officer that they were his workers. They, too, were allowed to join us.

From a distance I could see Ucek and Zarenka, my little neighbour friends, standing in the square with their parents and the other people who were to be sent away. A short time later, as we were moving out of the courtyard, Mrs Friedmann managed somehow to push Ucek and Zarenka towards my mother, their 'Aunt Gerda', pleading with her to 'save them, please save them!' The children ran over to us. My parents immediately moved towards the middle of our group in order to hide Ucek and Zarenka among all the grown-ups. The two children cried silently as we left the square. My mother tried to console them by whispering that they would soon see their parents again. That was not to be, for all those who were forced to remain in that square and the others who had already been evacuated earlier in the day, including my grandparents, were transported to Treblinka and killed on arrival in that extermination camp. In all, more than 20,000 people – almost the entire Jewish community of Kielce – were massacred in that operation.

Those of us who were not sent to Treblinka when the ghetto was liquidated ended up in an *Arbeitslager* – a labour camp – which occupied a small area of the former ghetto. The two or three streets that comprised the camp abutted what might once have been a large playground or park. When we got there, though, it was just an empty and dusty plot of land. Our family, with Ucek and Zarenka now part of it, was housed in a large room, with a kitchen and bathroom that we had to share with another family. The bathroom had a big tub in which we three children got a chance to be bathed from time to time. Here I was very happy because I now had a brother and a sister; not only that, I was the big brother and could lord it over them.

We arrived at the labour camp in the late autumn of 1942 – I was eight at the time – and remained there for about a year. My father still ran the *Werkstatt* while my mother struggled to feed the five of us on the meagre rations we were allowed, which was not easy. Except for the fact that our family had grown and that Ucek and Zarenka were my constant companions, only two events from our life in the labour camp stand out in my mind.

One day my mother received an order from the commandant of either the Gestapo or the Schutzpolizei summoning her to present herself at his office the next morning. She spent the remainder of the day in a terribly worried state, crying much of the time. When my father heard of the summons on his return that evening he turned pale and, while he told her not to worry, I could see that he, too, was very concerned. They kept wondering all evening why the commandant would want to see my mother and what would happen to her. 'Do you think that it has something to do with the children?' she asked. 'That's not it,' my father assured her. 'They would simply have come and dragged the children away.' More speculation followed and then my father said that he had figured it out and that they would talk about it later. At that point I started to cry because I thought that the Germans were going to kill my mother.

That night I heard my father and mother continue to whisper about the order she had received. My father explained that he was sure the Germans wanted her to become an informer. There could be no other reason for this strange summons, he claimed. If they had wanted to punish her for something, they would simply have come for her and that would have been the end of it. No, he was sure that they wanted to use her as an informer because, among other things, she spoke German and they could communicate directly with her. The problem was, my father explained, that if they told her what they wanted her to do and she refused, they would kill her or send her to Auschwitz or some other concentration camp. And if she did as they asked, she would eventually suffer the same fate. What to do? My father saw only one way out: 'Don't let them tell you what they want you to do. Just keep changing the subject. Talk about Göttingen, about anything, but for heaven's sake, don't let them tell you that they want you to work for them.'

The next day my mother was picked up and taken to the office of the commandant. I thought I would never see her again, and when Ucek and Zarenka saw me crying, they began to cry too and kept asking when Mutti was coming back. But she did return, and seemed much happier. When my father arrived that evening she greeted him with a big smile and a kiss. 'You were right,' she said. 'They wanted me to spy for them, but I never let the commandant get to the point. He must think that I am a babbling idiot and that I am too stupid to be of any use to them.'

The other event that has stayed with me is the liquidation of the labour camp. It began early one morning. The Germans drove into the camp, ordered everybody out into the street and herded us towards the big field in the middle of the camp. There we had to line up in two long columns, a dozen abreast. The two columns were separated by a gap of some five metres. When we had been properly lined up, the soldiers (I believe both the Schutzpolizei and Gestapo participated in this operation) began to walk up and down between the two columns, looking for children. The entire operation was overseen by the German city commandant. He stood in front, facing the two columns at a distance of about ten metres. From time to time he would bark out some order to his subordinates or flick his riding boots with a short horsewhip.

All around us children were being torn from the arms of their parents. When the soldiers saw Zarenka and Ucek they tried to wrest them away from my mother. The two children began to scream and my mother tried to hold on to them, but one of the soldiers began to beat her and she had to let go. Then one of the soldiers saw me and tried to drag me out as well. Holding on to me, my father stepped forward. As the soldier was getting ready to beat him as well, my father bellowed something and the man stopped. Still holding me by the hand, my father walked up to the city commandant. Before my father could say anything, I looked up at the commandant and said (I don't know why, perhaps it was at my father's prompting), 'Herr Hauptmann, ich kann arbeiten' – 'Captain, I can work.' He looked at me for a brief moment and said, 'Na, das werden wir bald sehen' – 'Well, that we'll soon get to see.' Then he motioned my father and me back towards the column where we had been standing.

We learned later that Ucek and Zarenka, with about thirty other children, were first locked up in a nearby house. From there, in the late afternoon, they were taken to the Jewish cemetery, where they were killed. We heard afterwards that the soldiers used hand grenades to murder them. In that cemetery in Kielce stands a monument erected in memory of the children who were killed on that terrible day in 1943, among them my little brother and sister. That is what they had become and that is what they will always be as long as I live. Over the years I have managed to erase from my memory many a horrendous experience in the camps, but never for a moment have I been able to forget the day when Ucek and Zarenka were taken from us.

What prompted the city commandant to spare my life on that morning has remained a mystery to me. Was it that I was blond and spoke fluent German and possibly reminded him of his own children? I shall never know.

After the liquidation of the labour camp we were divided into two groups and sent to two different factory complexes on the outskirts of Kielce. One group, comprising a few hundred people, went to Ludwików, a large foundry. My parents and I, as part of a similarly sized group, ended up in Henryków, a large sawmill that manufactured wooden wagons for the German war effort. The iron rims for the wheels of the wagons made in Henryków were produced in Ludwików. In Henryków we lived in a big barrack with all the other workers. My mother, father and I slept in bunks towards the back end of the barrack, separated from our neighbours by a thin curtain. I do not remember whether the *Werkstatt* was still in existence and whether my father still ran it, but I think it more likely that he now worked full-time at some machine in the factory. My mother served as a nurse in the small infirmary presided over by Dr Leon Reitter, the only doctor to be spared when all the Jewish doctors who survived the liquidation of the ghetto had been executed in the labour camp a few months before the children were murdered.

Soon I, too, had a job. My parents were afraid that the German officer who had let me live because I told him I could work might one day come to Henryków on an inspection tour and ask about me. Since I had not been assigned a job in the factory, my parents decided that I should try to get the German head of Henryków, a civilian manager by the name of Fuss, to hire me as his errand boy. In order to speak to Fuss, I waited for him one day outside the small house in which he had his office and approached him as he came out. When I told him what I wanted and that I also spoke Polish, he looked me up and down and, just when I was sure that he was not going to hire me, he said that he could use me. That's how I became his errand boy.

My job consisted mainly of taking the mail to a special mailbox, running various errands for Fuss on the factory grounds and parking the bicycles of the Germans who visited him from time to time. It did not take me long to figure out that these Germans were non-commissioned officers who did not qualify for the cars the higher Gestapo and Schutzpolizei officers came in. I feared the latter and tried to avoid them as much as possible. The ones on bikes seemed less threatening, although I knew from experience that any German in a uniform was better avoided. Whenever these men arrived at the building that housed Fuss's office, I had to take their bicycles and place them in the bike rack twenty or thirty metres away. At first I pushed the bikes obediently to the bike rack. Gradually I began to ride them like a scooter, with one foot on a pedal. As time went on and I became surer of myself, I would try to ride them. I was much too short, though: my feet could barely reach the pedals. Never having learned to ride a bike, naturally I fell off a few times, and while I did not mind a few scratches here and there on my hands or knees, I was afraid that I might damage the bikes and get into serious trouble. These were sturdy military cycles and could withstand considerable rough treatment, but had their owners or Fuss caught me trying to ride them I would certainly have been severely punished. That never happened, and I eventually got the hang of riding without falling off. Later, when teaching my sons to ride a bike, I often wondered whether they realised that there were more perilous ways of mastering the art than to have a father hold on to the saddle until he thought that it was safe to let go.

Fuss was in the habit of walking through the factory halls and yards with a whip. When he saw prisoners who were not working he would beat them severely with his whip. He administered these beatings indiscriminately to men and women alike, frequently injuring his victims quite badly. After seeing one such beating I decided to try to alert the workers whenever Fuss was on his way. As soon as I saw that my boss was getting ready to make one of his rounds, and if I did not have other chores to perform, I would run ahead of him through the factory halls. Since Fuss usually wore a Bavarian hat with a feather, I would signal his imminent arrival by wiggling my finger at the top of my head. I got a big kick out of performing this service and probably saved many a prisoner from a beating.

In the evenings I would tell my mother and father what I had been doing that day as Fuss's errand boy. On one occasion I mentioned that I could hear the radio broadcasts Fuss listened to in his office. He usually had the volume turned quite high, and when I sat in the corridor near his door I had no trouble hearing everything being said. Once I even heard Hitler speak; I was sure that it was Hitler because the person sounded just like my father when he did a Hitler imitation for our closest friends. That was a very dangerous thing to do, and my mother always warned him that someone might denounce him to the

Gestapo, but my father seemed to relish doing it. My report about the radio broadcasts prompted my father to suggest that I listen very carefully, try to memorise as much as possible what I heard, and report to him in the evening all I could remember. That became my regular assignment. Thereafter, whenever I had a chance, I would listen to Fuss's radio and sometimes also to what he and his visitors were talking about. One day I thought I heard that Mussolini had been captured by partisans. Since I knew that Mussolini was Hitler's friend, I could barely wait to tell my father all about it. For a while no one would believe me, but then the news was confirmed by some Polish workers who were regular employees at Henryków. From then on my reports on what was being broadcast on German radio were eagerly awaited. But our joy over Mussolini's capture was short lived, for we soon learned that he had been rescued by the Germans.

The perimeter of the Henryków factory was guarded by soldiers who, we were told, were Tatars. They must have gone over from the Soviet side to the German when taken prisoner and were serving in German auxiliary units. They were not heavily armed, which apparently prompted some young men in our barrack to believe that it would be easier to escape when the Tatars were on duty. One night some of these prisoners cut through the barbed-wire fence. The Tatars, who always struck us as less committed to guard duty than their German counterparts, nevertheless spotted the attempted breakout. They shot and killed one of the escaping prisoners on the spot and captured the others. We were, of course, awakened by all the shooting and screaming. The next morning the Tatars turned the prisoners over to the Gestapo, who drove away with them. Some days later, after gallows had been erected in front of our barrack, the prisoners, badly beaten and barely able to walk, were brought out. We had to line up and watch the hangings. The prisoners were ordered to stand on chairs under the gallows while the Germans forced an equal number of inmates, standing on ladders, to pull the noose over the hoodless heads of the condemned. I could see that the hands of one of the inmates were shaking violently as he struggled to put the rope over the prisoner's head. The prisoner turned and kissed the man's hand, said something to him and slid his head through the noose. The Gestapo officer in charge of the execution saw what had happened and furiously kicked the chair out from under the prisoner. It was obvious to us that the valour of the condemned man had robbed the German officer of much of the pleasure he must have expected to derive from his death. As I watched this horribly tragic scene, I was gripped by a curiously perverse sense of *Schadenfreude*, for it was only on very rare occasions that we could claim to spoil the pleasure the Gestapo appeared to derive from tormenting us, and this was one such occasion.

The bodies of the prisoners were left hanging for a few days near the entrance to the barrack as a warning against further escape attempts. There were to be other executions in Henryków – as time went on, they became routine – but I remember only the first. The dignity and humanity the young prisoner demonstrated moments before his death – and the disdainful refusal of the other condemned men to plead for their lives – no doubt served over time to reinforce my conviction that moral resistance in the face of evil is no less courageous than physical resistance, a point that has unfortunately been frequently lost in the debate over the lack of greater Jewish resistance during the Holocaust.

Our life at Henryków came abruptly to an end one morning in July 1944, almost a year after we got there. A large contingent of German soldiers entered Henryków and ordered all of us to line up in front of the barrack. Then we were marched under heavy guard to what I believe was the freight depot at Kielce. When we got there we found that the prisoners who had ended up in Ludwików when the labour camp was liquidated were there too. A freight train was already waiting for us and we were all ordered to get in. The doors were then locked from the outside. There was little light in the wagons, although we could look out between the slats on either side. I saw that the last car of the train was an open cattle truck bristling with heavy machine guns pointing in all directions. A soldier with a sub-machine gun sat in a little cab above each car.

As we were boarding the train we heard various announcements over the loudspeaker. One informed us that our next destination would be a factory in Germany where our labour was needed. This announcement was greeted with considerable relief and seemed, for a while, to silence the whispered rumours that we were on our way to Auschwitz. While I could not quite imagine what Auschwitz was really like, I had heard terrible stories about it, and I could sense that the mere mention of the name sent shivers down the backs of my parents and the other grown-ups.

Many hours passed as the train moved through the Polish countryside. Asked where he thought we were being taken, my father assured everybody in our car that the train appeared to be moving towards Germany. Having studied at the university in Kraków, not far from Auschwitz, my father knew that part of the country well. Some time later I heard my father whisper to my mother that the train had changed course and was moving in the direction of the concentration camp. Others soon realised what was happening. People began to cry and pray, others huddled together in whispered conversations. I remember my father taking a big gulp from a small bottle of vodka before passing it to my mother. My mother kept squeezing my hand and hugging me from time to time.

Two of our fellow prisoners started to pry open some floorboards in the middle of the car. Similar escape plans were apparently being hatched in other cars. As it got dark and while the train was travelling near a forested area, machine-gun fire, coming from the last car, exploded all around us. Our guards must have spotted those who were trying to escape by sliding through the holes in the floor of the cars and lying flat between the rails. We never found out whether any of the prisoners made it. The train did not stop and the shooting continued for some time. I think there were further attempts at escape, for we heard more gunfire, but the rest of us resigned ourselves to the fact that we would soon be arriving in Auschwitz.

Chapter 4

# Auschwitz

I was ten years old on that sunny morning in the first days of August 1944 when our train approached the outskirts of Auschwitz concentration camp. Actually, as we were to find out later, we were on our way to Birkenau, located a few kilometres down the road from Auschwitz proper. It was in Birkenau that the gas chambers and crematoriums had been erected, and it was here that millions of human beings died. Auschwitz was merely the public front for the Birkenau extermination camp. Auschwitz was shown to visiting dignitaries, whereas Birkenau was the last place on earth many of the prisoners sent there were destined to see.

As the train moved closer and closer to Birkenau we could see hundreds of people in striped prison uniforms digging ditches, carrying bricks, pushing heavy carts or marching in formation in different directions. '*Menschen!*' ('Human beings!') I heard someone mutter, and I sensed a collective sigh of relief in our car. *After all, they do not kill everybody on arrival*, must have been the thought that flashed through everyone's mind. The mood in the car lightened somewhat and people began to talk again. 'Maybe Auschwitz is not as bad as it has been made out to be,' somebody said. I thought that it looked just like Henryków, only bigger, and that it would not be all that bad.

Years later, when asked about Auschwitz and what it was like, I would reply that I was lucky to get into Auschwitz. This response would invariably produce a shocked look on the face of the person who had asked the question. But I really meant what I said. Most people who arrived at the Birkenau rail platform had to undergo a so-called selection. Here the children, the elderly and the invalids were separated from the rest of the people in their transport and taken directly to the gas chambers. Our group was spared the selection process. The SS officers in charge must not have ordered it because they probably assumed, since our transport came from a labour camp, that children and others not able to work had already been eliminated. Had there been a selection, I would have been killed before ever making it into the camp. That is what I meant with my flippant remark about being lucky to get into Auschwitz.

Of course, when we arrived in Birkenau I did not know what to expect, nor that I had escaped the deadly selection process. As soon as we stepped out of our wagons on to the station platform, all men were ordered to line up on one side and women on the other. But for one brief moment a few months later, this was the last time I was to see my mother until we were reunited on 29 December 1946, almost two and a half years after our separation. We could not say goodbye properly because the SS guards were constantly yelling for us to move, hitting and kicking anyone who did not immediately do as they were ordered. I was too scared to cry or even to wave to her and stayed close to my father.

My father held on to me as we were marched away from the station towards a big building. Here we were ordered to take off our clothes and made to run through some showers and a disinfecting foot pool. Along the way our hair was shorn off and we were thrown the same blue-and-white striped prison uniforms we had seen from the train. It was at this point that my father whispered to me that we had made it, for only when we had received the uniforms could he be sure we were not being taken to the gas chambers.

With that process behind us we were again ordered to line up and march. We must have walked for quite some time before we came upon rows and rows of barracks as far as the eye could see. Streets – actually unpaved roads – cut through the rows while high barbed-wire fences divided what looked like a large town into sizeable individual camps, each with its own gate and guard towers. Later I was to learn that these individual camps were identified by letters. Women were housed in camps B and C, men in camp D, and so on. Our destination was camp E, better known as the Gypsy camp. That camp had housed many thousands of Gypsy families. All of them – men, women and children – were murdered shortly before we arrived. Only the name remained to remind us of yet another horrendous crime committed in the name of the master race.

The entrance to the Gypsy camp, consisting of a movable barbed-wire gate, was guarded by the SS with their dogs. Once inside we were ordered to line up in single file behind a group of barracks and made to roll up our left sleeves. At one end of the line two inmates sat at a wooden table. Each of us had to move up to the table, state our name and stretch out our left arm. I was walking ahead of my father in the line, wondering what would happen next. Then I saw that the men at the table held what looked like pens with a thin needle, and that they were writing something on the outstretched arms after dunking the pens in an inkpot: we were being tattooed. When my turn came I was afraid that it would hurt, but it was done so quickly that I could hardly feel it. Now I had a new name: B-2930, and it was the only 'name' that mattered here. The number, faded now, is still there on my left arm. It remains a part of me and serves as a reminder, not so much of my past, but of the obligation I deem incumbent on me, as a witness and survivor of Auschwitz, to fight the ideologies of hate and of racial and religious superiority that have for centuries caused so much suffering to humankind.

My father, who was right behind me in the tattoo line, became B-2931. Our numbers were also printed on a strip of cloth with a yellow triangle, the colour identifying us as Jews. (There were different colours to distinguish between different types of inmates. Political prisoners, for example, were given red triangles. Other colours were assigned to homosexuals, criminals, and so on.) Forty-five years later, when I returned to Auschwitz and gave the person in charge of the archives my name in order to find out when precisely I had arrived there in 1944, she asked for my number. I looked surprised, since I had always believed that the Germans kept very precise records in their camps. 'By the time you arrived,' she explained, 'there was such a large influx of new arrivals that the SS no longer bothered to record the names of inmates, only their numbers.' Sure enough, once she had my number, she was able to provide the dates I needed. The card with my number even disclosed how many people had come with me to Auschwitz from Kielce. It occurred to me then that, unlike those of us who survived Auschwitz and can by reference to their numbers document their existence in that camp, those prisoners who died in its crematoriums after the SS had stopped recording their names have left behind no trace of their presence in that terrible place. No bodies and no names, only ashes and nameless numbers. It is hard to imagine a greater affront to human dignity.

After we had been tattooed we were assigned barracks. Ours was a wooden structure like all the others in the Gypsy camp, with a mud floor that divided two long rows of wide, three-tier wooden bunks. Once inside we were greeted by a burly prisoner with a cane. This, I was to learn right away, was the *Blockältester* or barrack boss. He kept pointing to the bunks and yelling in Polish and Yiddish, 'Ten men to each level!' Whoever did not move fast enough for him was hit or kicked. My father and I found a bunk, picked the middle level and were soon joined by eight other inmates. Then we were ordered to lie on our stomachs with our heads pointing towards the middle of the room. I can't recall whether we were given blankets, but I am sure that we had no mattresses.

Although we were not given anything to eat that evening, the very thought of food was forced from my mind by what happened later. Into the barrack strutted two or three well-fed inmates with canes and clubs. They wore armbands bearing the word *Kapo*. Kapos were inmates who, together with the barrack bosses, ran the camp for the SS and terrorised their fellow inmates day in, day out. Right after the kapos had greeted our barrack boss, one of them yelled in German, 'Spiegel, you son of a bitch, get down. We want to talk to you!' As soon as Spiegel stood before them, the men surrounded him and started to hit him with their fists and clubs: on his face, his head, his legs, his arms. The more Spiegel begged for mercy and screamed, the more the kapos beat him. From what I could make out as the kapos yelled while beating him, Spiegel had apparently denounced one of them to the Gestapo in Kielce, with the result that he had been sent to Auschwitz two years earlier.

Spiegel was soon on his knees and then flat on the ground, begging to be allowed to die. He was covered with blood and no longer really trying to protect himself against the blows that continued to rain down on him. The kapos then picked Spiegel up and began to push and pull him out of the barrack. We did not see what happened next, but we heard that the kapos had dragged him to the fence and that he died on it. Our camp, like the others in Birkenau, was enclosed by a high-voltage electric fence that emitted a perennial buzz. The fence separated those of us in the Gypsy camp from camp D on one side and camp F on the other. A single wire strung about a metre high and a metre from the fence on either side warned inmates not to get any closer lest they be electrocuted. Spiegel must have died after being thrown against the fence, or after crawling into it. Gradually, I came to realise that it was not uncommon for inmates to commit suicide by what was known as 'walking into the fence'.

It is difficult not to wonder whether it ever occurred to these kapos that they were no different from Spiegel. He denounced fellow Jews to the Gestapo because he believed that he was thereby prolonging his own life, whereas the kapos allowed themselves to become the surrogates of the SS by beating their fellow inmates, forcing them to work to total exhaustion and depriving them of their rations, knowing full well that such actions would hasten their deaths. And all that in order to improve the kapos' own chances of survival. Besides testing the morality of those who became neither informers nor kapos, the concentration camps were laboratories for the survival of the brutish. Both Spiegel and the kapo had been friends of my parents. Both had been with us in Katowice. At that time they had been my 'uncles'. I seem to recall that the kapo whom

Spiegel had denounced had been a dental technician or dentist in his prior life; I never knew what Spiegel's profession had been. Had they not ended up in the camps, they probably would have remained decent human beings. What is it in the human character that gives some individuals the moral strength not to sacrifice their decency and dignity, regardless of the cost to themselves, whereas others become murderously ruthless in the hope of ensuring their own survival?

I remember very little about my activities in the days immediately following the beating of Spiegel. Of course, I thought a lot about my mother and missed her very much. I wondered what she was doing, whether they had also cut off her hair as they had ours, whether she had enough to eat and whether she had to live in a barrack similar to ours. In those early days I was also introduced to the Auschwitz feeding system. We would be awakened early in the morning and made to line up in front of a big kettle from which an inmate with a ladle would serve a liquid that looked like black coffee. Next to him stood the barrack boss, cutting slices of black bread. The bread was frequently mouldy and the slices rather small. I soon noticed that not everyone got the same amount of bread. Those the barrack boss did not like would get a smaller piece or no bread at all, while his friends and he himself would keep whole loaves. Complaints would invite a beating. In the evening we would be served the day's only other meal. It consisted, as a rule, of some tasteless, watery turnip soup. Since we got no bread in the evening, I would try to save a little piece of my morning bread for later in the day, hiding it very carefully so that it would not be stolen.

That, more or less, was all we had to eat. On such a diet some people gradually became 'Muselmans', the name given to inmates who had become so emaciated that they walked around in a stupor, stopped eating altogether and in no time died quietly. I soon learned that anyone who became a Muselman would not live very long. That was the fate of a friend of my parents whom I had called 'uncle' for as long as I could remember. He and his wife had been with us in Katowice. He was Jewish, she was not. And while, as a German Gentile, she could have left him and gone back to Germany, she refused to do so and helped him as best she could. In Kielce, she lived outside the ghetto and somehow managed to get food to him; she did the same in the labour camp. I still remember them talking over the fence in the ghetto. Access to Auschwitz or anywhere near the camp was closed to her and he, a big man, simply could not live on the rations we received. When I saw him a few weeks after we had arrived in Auschwitz, he was the skinniest human being I had ever seen. He no longer recognised my father or me and kept mumbling to himself. After the war my mother and I visited his wife, who had returned to her native Hamburg. Understandably, she wanted to know when I had last seen her husband and whether I knew what had happened to him. I lied and told her that the last time I had seen him he had been his usual friendly self, although somewhat thinner. I simply could not bring myself to tell this woman, whom we all admired for her courage and loyalty to her husband, the truth about his last days. She had suffered enough.

I do not remember how long my father and I remained in the barrack we occupied when we first arrived in the Gypsy camp. One of the kapos who took part in the terrible beating of Spiegel was in charge of a barrack that served as a kind of warehouse, where the clothing taken from people on their arrival in Auschwitz was sorted and eventually shipped out. Where it went, I never found out. To help us, the kapo had my father and me and a few of his other friends from Kielce assigned to his barrack. We slept there and worked there. In many ways this was a life-saving break for us. We were no longer subjected to the maltreatment dished out in our original barrack, we had a little more food, and our bunk bed had blankets and a straw mattress. Equally important, we could keep warm with some of the clothes stored in the barrack.

In our new barrack my father and I shared a bunk with my friend Walter and his step-father. Walter had managed to avoid being murdered with the children of Kielce because he was a few years older than most of them and was rather tall. After we had moved into our new barrack, Walter got very sick. His father took him to the infirmary, where he was admitted after being diagnosed with diphtheria. The barracks serving as the infirmary of the Gypsy camp were located diagonally opposite our barrack. Less than a week after Walter had entered the infirmary we were awakened one night by terrible noises coming from across the street. SS trucks with their motors running were standing outside the infirmary while SS guards herded screaming patients into the trucks. The patients knew that they were being taken to the gas chambers, and we knew that the SS was thinning out the population of the infirmary to make room for new admissions. They would do that every few weeks; that is why it was so dangerous to get sick. In the morning we learned that Walter was among those who had been taken away. His step-father kept blaming himself for Walter's death because he had taken him to the infirmary, but we all knew that he had had no choice, given Walter's illness. I still do not understand how it was possible for Walter to come down with diphtheria while I, sleeping next to him, escaped infection. Was it just luck, or is it possible that he did not really have this highly contagious disease?

Every few weeks the SS would enter the Gypsy camp and embark on its periodic selections. These selections were usually conducted by one or two SS doctors, most often under the supervision of the infamous Dr Mengele, known as the Angel of Death, whose very name made me tremble with fear. The selections would take place early in the morning, after all the inmates had been lined up in front of their barracks and counted. Even when there was no selection, the daily counting process was an ordeal that could last for hours, particularly when someone appeared to be missing. The missing person usually turned out to be an inmate who had died overnight. The daily head count was frequently accompanied by beatings and at times also by hangings. Soon after we arrived in Auschwitz my father, seeing how routine selections were conducted and that children were most at risk, came up with a strategy to beat the system. Every morning when we had to line up for the daily count I would try to stand as far back as possible and very close to the entrance of the barrack. As soon as we had been counted and if it appeared that there might be a selection, I would try to slip back into the barrack and hide. That manoeuvre saved me a number of times. It was not always easy to execute, however, because I had to disappear without being seen by the SS or the barrack boss, but I was never caught.

Selections were sometimes also conducted at random. Mengele would enter the camp with some of his assistants and order any children or sick or old people he encountered in the barracks or walking outside to be taken away. My father discussed this problem with our kapo friend, who suggested that a real job might afford me some protection. A few days later I was hired to serve as errand boy for the kapo of the sauna, as the camp's bathhouse was called. Here newly arrived inmates from other sub-camps were given a walk-through shower and had their clothes disinfected. My job – I think now that it may have been created as a favour to my father's friend – consisted mainly of running errands for my new boss. Whenever an SS guard stopped me somewhere in the camp, which happened from time to time, I would identify myself as the sauna's errand boy and be permitted to be on my way. The job gave me a greater sense of security than I had before when meeting up with an SS guard, although it was always hard not to tremble when called over by one of them.

At times I would have to deliver a message or package to someone at another camp. I try in vain to recall how I was able to leave and come back, but I remember being sent once, together with another person, to one of the crematoriums (we used that term generically to refer to both the gas chambers and the crematoriums themselves). We had to pick up the gas my sauna boss needed for the disinfection of clothes. Naturally, I was terribly afraid to go near the place, but had to do it anyway. When we got there we were greeted by inmates who worked at the crematoriums. Their job was to remove the bodies from the gas chambers and burn them in the crematoriums. They were all strong young men who joked around with us, probably because they sensed that we were terrified to be so close to the gas chambers. After we told them what we had come for, they gave us some containers of gas to take back to the sauna. The person who had accompanied me thought that we had been given the same Zyklon-B gas that was used to kill people in the gas chambers. I have no way of knowing whether that was true, although it made some sense, considering that we got it from the crematorium.

The air in Auschwitz always smelled foul because of the smoke that came out of the crematorium chimneys. The odour and smoke became stronger with every new transport that arrived in Birkenau, because the people who could not pass the initial selection process on the station platform were immediately herded into the gas chambers. Whenever the crematoriums were being operated at night, the sky above them would take on a reddish-brown colour. One summer, many decades after the war, I visited Auschwitz and saw birds and wild flowers in what used to be Birkenau. It suddenly struck me that I had never seen a bird before in the camp. The smoke must have kept them away. Nor can I remember seeing any grass or trees there. The soil turned to mud when it rained and remained mud for days on end, except in the winter when a mixture of dirty snow and ice covered the ground.

There was one barrack in the Gypsy camp where we could wash. Its water, always a rusty brown colour and always ice cold, came streaming out from small holes drilled in the long pipes which hung above sinks that resembled feeding troughs for cattle. Another barrack served as a communal toilet. There, holes cut into long rows of elevated concrete slabs served as toilet seats. This was our favourite camp location because it was the only place where it was always warm. But we were never allowed to stay there longer than a few minutes. This rule was strictly enforced by an inmate caretaker from Greece. I will never forget him. He played the mandolin very beautifully when not chasing us out. I soon worked out that if I told him that I loved his music, he would let me stay a little longer in that warm toilet.

One day, it may well have been in late October, we were awakened for what appeared to be a selection, although it differed from the previous ones I was familiar with. We had no idea what was happening, since the SS was not following its routine selection procedures. Instead of being counted as usual on such occasions, we were lined up, barrack by barrack, and herded into another barrack towards one end of the camp. Once inside we had to move in single file past a group of doctors who stood facing us at the end of the room. I believe Mengele was there, but I cannot be sure since I never really dared to look. SS guards were posted a few metres apart the entire length of the barrack and on either side of the panel of doctors. My father walked in first and I followed behind him, looking for an escape route. There was none. When we were just a few metres away from the doctors, one of them motioned my father to the left and me to the right. My father tried to pull me with him, but an SS guard grabbed me while another kicked my father out of the barrack. That was the last time I saw my father.

I was taken to an adjacent barrack. It was guarded by an inmate who must have been the barrack boss. When I arrived in that room some other people were already there. Most of them looked sick, others were old and some had become Muselmans or were close to it. There was another entrance at the end of the room. That door was kept closed with a piece of wire. Seeing my opportunity, I stationed myself close to the door and waited. More people were brought into our room, all no different from those already there. They seemed resigned to their fate. I was not! I knew that our destination was the gas chamber and that I had to find a way to escape in order to rejoin my father. Moving ever closer to the door and keeping my eye on the barrack boss, I began to unwind the wire. It came apart rather easily and I bolted out of the door. Behind me I could hear some fellow inmates yell that I was escaping. Alerted, the barrack boss raced out and caught me. He slapped me around a few times and dragged me back to the barrack. I managed to get out of the room twice more, but was caught each time and given a few more blows.

At that point I decided that I would not be able to escape and that in a few hours I would die in the gas chamber. At first I was terribly angry with my fellow inmates who had given me away each time I had tried to escape. I could not understand why they had done that. My escape would certainly not have affected their fate, and they must have known that they were on their way to the gas chamber. Then I thought of my father and how upset he must be because, unlike in the past, he had not been able to avoid letting me get caught in a selection. I would have liked to have been able to tell him that he should not blame himself, for he could not possibly have anticipated the trap we had walked into.

With these thoughts still swirling in my head, I moved to a corner of the room, away from the door, and sat down. After a few minutes, I realised that I could no longer hear any voices around me, nor the barked orders of the SS guards in the nearby barrack. Until then I had been gripped with fear, fear of dying, for I knew that, having failed to escape, I was on my way to the gas chamber. But then something most unusual happened. Slowly, very slowly, my fear and anxiety faded away as I admitted to myself that there was no way out and that I would die in a few hours. The nervous tension that had hung over me like a cloud lifted. An inner warmth streamed through my body. I was at peace, my fear had vanished and I was no longer afraid of dying.

When the selection had ended, there were some thirty to forty inmates in the room. We sat there waiting for the truck that would take us to the gas chamber. Nothing happened for a while, and then an SS lorry rolled up and we were ordered inside. At first it headed in the direction of the crematoriums, but then it veered off and entered the nearby *Krankenlager*, or hospital camp, which housed prisoners who were sick or quarantined (I believe this was camp F). The truck rolled up to one of the barracks and we were ordered out. Here we were received by orderlies who took down our numbers on small index cards and made some other notations on each of them. When pressed to tell us why we had been brought to them, they told us that we were there 'in transit'. The SS had apparently concluded that it would be a waste of resources to take our small group to the gas chamber, which would also have meant firing up one of the crematoriums. They decided instead to keep us in this camp until they had put together a larger group.

The barrack in which we were housed held inmates with a skin disease: scabies, or *Krätze* in German. They appeared to have scabs all over their bodies and scratched all the time. Every morning they would line up, be inspected by a young

Polish doctor and usually be given an orange salve. I was afraid that I would catch the disease and went to see the doctor a few times as a precaution. He was always very kind to me and gave me advice on how to avoid coming down with scabies. On one occasion he handed me a piece of soap – it had been quite a while since I had seen soap – and told me to wash my hands frequently. Every so often he would examine me and express delight that I remained free from infection. He made sure that I always had enough soap. From time to time he also slipped me some bread and arranged for me to be moved to a corner bunk at the other end of the barrack, away from the entrance and those areas where the other inmates tended to congregate.

Once I was pretty sure that I wasn't going to get scabies, I began to like my life in the hospital camp. *Maybe the SS forgot us,* I thought hopefully, and, for a while, it seemed that that was what had happened. The only really unpleasant part about being in that barrack was its proximity to the crematoriums. Many a night I would wake up to screams and pleas for help from people being herded into the gas chambers. It was terrible. At first I would lie awake shaking. Then, when I fell asleep, I would have nightmares, terribly scary and vivid nightmares in which I was being beaten or executed. They made me afraid to sleep because the same dreams kept returning night after night. After a while, without realising what was happening, I had found a way to cope with them: in my sleep, while the nightmare was upon me, I would hear myself say, 'This is only a nightmare, there is nothing to be afraid of.' And the nightmare would vanish. After that, whenever I was half-awakened by the horrified screams coming from the nearby gas chambers, my mind would unconsciously transform them into nightmares, and I would continue to sleep.

So one night, when I kept hearing terrified voices all around me, I went right on sleeping, believing that I was again having one of my nightmares. But when I woke up the next morning I was told that the SS had come during the early hours and dragged out all the people who had been brought to this barrack with me. But why hadn't they taken me too? *It was a miracle*, I thought. Soon, though, I learned why I had been spared. When we had first arrived at the *Krankenlager* a red X had been placed on the back of our individual index cards. My friend the young Polish doctor had apparently torn up my card and issued me a new one without the marking. When the SS came in and demanded the cards with the red Xs, mine was not among them. The doctor had saved my life, and my nightmares saved me from witnessing what was happening that night and possibly giving myself away.

I remained in the hospital camp for another week or two. Then one day the doctor called me to his little cubicle and told me that I was to be moved to the children's barrack in camp D. Having learned to be suspicious – not of him, of course, but of the people with whom he had arranged my transfer – I kept asking him how he could be sure that my destination was camp D and not the gas chamber. He assured me that I had nothing to worry about. That turned out to be true. A few hours later I was taken to the children's barrack in camp D. To this day I don't really know how this transfer was arranged. All I remember is that I was picked up by an SS guard, the oldest SS guard I had ever seen. He did not look like the other SS guards I had encountered. They were usually young, seemed to pride themselves on their military bearing and appeared to enjoy mistreating us. This man was kind and kept telling me that I would like the children's barrack and that I would be safe there. He was the first SS guard in whose presence I did not fear for my life. Later I heard that by 1944 old men were being drafted into the SS because the young ones were needed at the front. It may well be that this SS guard was one of these draftees.

Before I was sent there, I had no idea that a children's barrack even existed. I was told later that it was the brainchild of a German political prisoner who had saved a group of teenagers from the gas chambers by convincing the SS that they could be put to better use working in the camp. The SS agreed to let him prove it and put him in charge of a barrack that housed only boys. In time, other boys ended up in that barrack. Most if not all of the kids in the children's barrack were older than I. Among them were two friends, Michael and Janek, whom I knew from Kielce. They had survived the murder of the children in the labour camp of Kielce by hiding in the attic of the house where the children were held before being taken to the cemetery. I was delighted to see them again and we soon became inseparable. Our common experience bonded us like brothers.

Garbage collection was the job to which most of the children were assigned. Sometimes we also had to collect from other camps. We would pick up the rubbish in various places, put it in wooden carts and take it to a dump. Three or four kids were usually assigned to a cart. Michael and Janek somehow managed to have me put on their team. In general, our work was not very difficult. But when it rained, which happened often, our shoes and the wheels of our cart would sink into the mud, making pushing it that much harder.

Once we ended up close to one of the women's camps. We were sent to pick up some garbage in camp C. It bordered on one side of our camp D. This enabled the men and women in these camps to engage in yelling conversations across the electrified fence. My father had found out that my mother was in camp B, which meant that we could not see her from our camp. But as soon as we had entered camp C, Michael, Janek and I, together with two other kids, began to push our cart close to the side of the fence that bordered on camp B. Whenever we saw any women on the other side, we yelled over to them in Polish and Yiddish that they should alert women from Kielce. A few minutes later, we recognised some women we knew from Kielce, among them relatives of Janek and Michael. Then I saw my mother. When she spotted me she began to cry and call, 'Tommy, Tommy!' And if others had not held her back, she would have tried to reach me through the electrified fence. All I could think of was that she was alive, while she kept repeating, 'Du *lebst, du lebst*!' ('You're alive!') Then she asked about my father. I began to tell her that my father had been shipped out on a transport, but a woman kapo raced over and chased all the women away from the fence. For months afterwards I kept replaying her words in my mind and seeing her tear-covered, smiling face across the fence. What mattered was that she was still alive and not a Muselman: she was thin, but looked well in the circumstances and, I kept saying to myself, she was very beautiful even without her hair. Not long after that encounter I heard that a large transport of female prisoners, my mother among them, had been moved to a camp in Germany.

Our barrack boss treated us well and distributed the rations fairly. Only rarely did the rations suffice to overcome that lingering feeling of hunger that had become part of me. Still, I always resisted eating anything we found in the garbage. Since we were also responsible for what was thrown out of the SS kitchen, the temptation was great to eat the remains of a sandwich or to lick a can that still contained a few slivers of food or some drops of soup or sauce. Whenever I saw such items I would remember my father's repeated warning never to eat anything from the garbage lest I get terribly sick. Once, though, a special opportunity presented itself. While collecting from outside the SS kitchen we looked through the open window and saw that it was empty. Near the stove stood a pan filled with milk. It had been years since Michael, Janek or I had tasted milk. We looked at each other and, without a word, Michael climbed through the kitchen window. He took a big gulp of milk, then passed the pan through the window to us. Janek and I took a few sips from the pan and handed it back to Michael. He put whatever was left of the milk back where he had found it and climbed out again as fast as he could. Had we been caught, our punishment would have been a very severe beating or worse. But we were not caught, and to this day I can still taste that heavenly mouthful of milk. No milk has ever tasted as good. Years later, when my own children would have to be coaxed to drink their milk, I would think of that day in the SS kitchen and be grateful that they never had to risk their lives to get it. At the same time I would have to hide my anger that they did not appreciate what it meant to have milk in abundance. But how could they? For many of us who survived the camps, food took on an almost mystical quality. Despite the fact that I am not religious, I consider it a sin to throw bread away, however stale it might have become, and will walk miles to feed it to birds or, remembering my job as Shabbat goy in Kielce, let my wife throw it away instead.

Not long after I had seen my mother, the older boys in our barrack reported in conspiratorial tones that there were rumours that the Germans were losing the war and that the Russians were approaching. I did not really know what to believe or what it all meant. The thought that we might soon be liberated never quite entered my consciousness. I could think only of the cold Polish winter that was upon us and the fact that it was ever more difficult to stay warm. It must have been late December 1944 or early January 1945. The soil under our feet was frozen. The mud was no longer a problem, but the ice made it hard not to slide while pushing the garbage carts. Of course, the garbage was also frozen and difficult to load. As we worked on breaking it up, we consoled ourselves with the thought that frozen garbage did not smell.

Then, one morning, we were awakened by repeated announcements coming at us in those harsh German command tones to which I never quite got accustomed: '*Das Lager wird geräumt!*' ('The camp is being evacuated!') We were ordered to line up in front of the barrack with all our possessions. Mine consisted of a thin blanket, a spoon and a metal container that served both as my cup and soup plate. I always had the cup tied by a string to the piece of rope that acted as my belt. Once assembled, we were marched through the main Birkenau gate. The road outside was already lined with thousands of inmates standing eight or ten abreast. 'Children to the front of the column!' came the order. Our barrack was to be in the lead. The column was so long that it took us quite some time to get to the front. It was freezing and a very strong wind was blowing through our clothes. As we stood there waiting, we were thrown a loaf of black bread. Then the order came: 'Forward, march!'

The Auschwitz Death March had begun.

*Chapter 5*

# The Auschwitz Death Transport

As we began to march, leaving Birkenau gradually behind us, I looked back towards the vast stretch of land with its hundreds of barracks, administrative buildings, guard towers and electrified fences. Further in the distance I could see the remains of the crematoriums that the SS had tried to demolish. I could not really believe that I was leaving this terrible place alive. I remembered what my father once said in the Ghetto of Kielce as he and a few friends shared a bottle of vodka: 'Do not despair. Sooner or later we will win this war and bury them deep under the ground.' And I could hear my mother trying to shush him by warning that 'the walls have ears'. But he would not be silenced. Years later I wondered whether my father really believed what he had said or whether it was vodka-induced optimism or just hope, or both. Now, as I looked back on this vast murder factory, I felt victorious and kept repeating to myself, as if addressing Hitler directly, 'See, you tried to kill me, but I am still alive!'

Of course, the march had only just begun and I had no idea what lay ahead. And what lay ahead turned out to be worse than anything I could have imagined. The roads were covered with snow and ice. It was January, after all, and a typical Polish winter. As the sun gradually set it became colder and colder. The trees along some of the roads gave us temporary protection against the icy wind that would blow against us and pass right through our thin clothes. I was wearing my mother's boots, which she had given me before we reached Auschwitz. My socks had been taken away when I had arrived at the camp. In their place I used some rags to keep my feet warm. Michael, Janek and I stayed close together, trying to keep warm. We were getting tired and realised that those of us from the children's barrack, having been ordered by the SS guards to the front of the column of marchers, had it harder than those who followed on the snow and ice we kids had trampled down. By late afternoon Janek, Michael and I were finding it increasingly difficult to keep up and decided to let the marchers pass us until the rear of the column was almost upon us. Then we jogged to the front again. Once we discovered that this manoeuvre worked, we kept repeating it. Of course, we were getting pushed aside or bumped by the marchers, but that was a small price to pay for the respite it gave us.

It was already dark when the SS halted the column for the night and allowed us to sleep on the road where we had stopped or in the drainage ditches on either side. By that time some of the marchers had already died. Those who could not go on and either sat down by the side of the road or simply collapsed were shot by the SS guards, who kicked their bodies into the nearest ditch. Over the next two days many more would die in this manner. After a while I would no longer flinch when yet another shot was fired. As I became ever more tired and the cold windy air began to hurt, I wondered whether it would not be easier to lie down by the side of the road and let them kill me too. The prospect had its attraction because it would be speedy and liberating. But I would almost immediately banish that thought and push myself even harder. 'If I give up, they will have won,' I kept muttering to myself. Staying alive had become a game I played against Hitler, the SS and the Nazi killing machine.

After marching for three days we reached Gliwice (Gleiwitz), a town seventy kilometres or so from Birkenau. These three days have become blurred in my mind, making it difficult for me to identify the specific day on which a given event occurred. For example I can no longer say with any degree of certainty whether it was towards the end of the first day or the second that the SS decided the children's barrack was slowing down the march. But I remember very clearly that it was just beginning to get dark when the guards halted the column and ordered the group from the children's barrack to the side of the road to be taken 'to rest in a nearby convent'. At that moment, Michael, Janek and I were not in front with the others from our barrack. Instead we were once again doing our rest-and-jog routine and had come to a stop near the middle of the column. Despite the orders of the SS for children to come forward, we decided to stay where we were. Some men around us tried to push us out, but we fought them off. The three of us had learned long ago not to trust the SS. 'Rest in a convent' sounded too good to be true. I was told later that our friends from the children's barrack had all been murdered. I do not know whether that is true, but I never saw any of them again.

A group of Russian prisoners of war were marching in formation in one part of the column. I had not seen them when we were leaving Auschwitz and thought that they might have joined our transport at some later point. They attracted my attention because it was never easy to get around them when Michael, Janek and I moved from one end of the column to the other. We were afraid of the Russians because we thought they kept jostling us in order to grab our bread. We held on to it as tightly as we could whenever we came close to them.

One evening the column was halted and we were all ordered to sit down on the road. Everybody but the Russians obeyed the order. They remained standing and began to sing what must have been a patriotic song. A guard blew a whistle and more than a dozen of his SS comrades materialised out of nowhere and moved towards the Russians. 'Alle hinlegen!' ('All down!') the officer in charge shouted. The Russians remained standing. Then the officer shouted something and the guards opened fire. They must have killed some of the Russians, for a number of them fell. The shooting continued until the survivors sat down. I can no longer recall, if I ever knew, what prompted this tragic episode. What I do remember, though, is that the standoff gave me an opportunity to rest and that I dozed off at some point with the shooting and screaming still ringing in my ears.

The next morning, after we had again spent the night sleeping on the road, I noticed that more people had died overnight and that others were too weak to continue. By then what was happening around me had become routine: the SS would kill those who refused to continue and order some nearby marchers to push the dead into the closest ditch. Increasingly I blocked these scenes from my consciousness and no longer registered what was happening around me. I seemed to be in a trance as I struggled to walk in order to stay alive.

In the mornings, as soon as Michael, Janek and I were fully awake, we would encourage each other to jump around and to rub our numb limbs. When I told them that I thought I could not feel my toes, Janek told me to wiggle them. I did, but that did not seem to help much. The cold was becoming unbearable. We ate our remaining bread and licked a few handfuls of snow. That was our breakfast. Oh, what I would have given for even a few spoonfuls of that terrible Auschwitz turnip soup or, for that matter, anything warm!

We reached Gliwice, a Silesian industrial centre, on the third day of our march and entered what appeared to be an empty labour camp. I began to fantasise that heated barracks, beds with blankets and even warm food awaited us. But I was almost immediately torn out of this dream world when we came to a stop at the edge of a run-down sports field. A group of SS officers stood in the middle of the field, which was ringed by a large number of heavily armed guards and their dogs. It did not take me long to realise that another selection awaited us: those among us who could jog to the other side of the field would live, the rest would be eliminated. By this time I could barely walk. Michael and Janek were not doing all that much better. We were exhausted, hungry and cold, but we wanted to live and we were not going to give up now after all we had been through on the march. As we looked out over the field we could see people trying to run across it; some appeared to collapse along the way or simply just sat down. Every so often the guards would come over and drag these unfortunates to the side of the field. When our turn came, we held hands to support each other and ran as fast as we could, which was not very fast at all. Dirty, with our torn clothes, we must have looked like beggar children emerging from a dark cellar. We could hear the SS officers laugh hilariously as the three of us passed. These hated voices invigorated us and gave us the strength we did not have just minutes earlier, and we made it across.

We must have stayed in Gliwice for a number of days. Here we were able to rest and recover some of our strength. The food was no better than that we had been given in Auschwitz, but at least we got some warm soup, and the portions of bread seemed a little larger. Just as I was beginning to believe that we would remain in Gliwice, we were ordered to march out of the camp and proceed to a nearby train station. Here open railcars, like those used for transporting coal or sand, awaited us. We were herded into these cars with so many other prisoners that there was hardly any room to move. Michael, Janek and I found ourselves being pressed against the taller grown-ups and could barely breathe. Above us, at one end of the car, sat a heavily armed SS guard in what looked like a brakeman's cabin. Since the cars had no roof, the SS guard could see what was happening and anticipate any escape attempts. I seem to remember that, before leaving, we were each given a loaf of black bread and a tin can that was supposed to contain meat. I never did find out what was in it since we had no can opener, knife or even a rock that would enable us to open it.

Our car was so crowded at first that, despite the fact that we were riding in open cars in January, Michael, Janek and I were kept warm by the bodies that pressed against us. After a day or two, to avoid being trampled, we decided to work our way towards a corner of the car. People were dying all around us and when our guard was asked what should be done with the bodies, he said to throw them out. That was being done with increasing frequency as the days went by. Our car was gradually becoming less crowded until it was no longer difficult to walk from one end to the other. The snow and wind seemed never to let up and we could feel the cold more now than before because there were fewer warm bodies pressing against us. Our bread was long gone, and all we had to eat was snow. We pretended that it was ice cream, although I doubt that we remembered what ice cream tasted like.

The nights in the car were horrendous. The hunger and cold

were wearing people down, not only physically but also mentally. Some began to hallucinate. They walked into the walls of the car, making noises like wild animals. They seemed to be seeing ghosts or monsters. They would fall over us or run into us and scream while waving their arms wildly as if trying to hit us. We soon noticed that these men seldom survived the night.

Just as I was thinking that it would surely be only a matter of a day or two before I, too, would die and be thrown overboard, a miracle occurred. As the train moved slowly through Czechoslovakia, making frequent stops, we began to see men, women and children standing on the bridges we passed under. They waved to us and shouted, and then loaves of bread began to fall into our train. Under the first bridge, Michael was able to catch a loaf and told me to hold on to it while he and Janek readied themselves for the next. I put the bread under my legs. When they came back, the bread was gone. Somebody had managed to steal it out from under me and I was too numb with cold to feel it. But we soon had more bread because the Czechs kept throwing it at us from the bridges. Had it not been for that Czech bread, we would not have survived. I never learned how this magnificent campaign had been mounted, but as long as I live, I will not forget these angels – to me they seemed to be angels – who provided us bread as if from heaven.

We were fortunate that the train could not take the shorter and more direct route from Gliwice to Germany, our final destination. By the end of January 1945 the Allies had severely damaged the German rail system, forcing our train to take the route through Czechoslovakia. That proved to be our salvation, although it is also true that, had the train been able to proceed directly to Germany, some of those prisoners who died while we were travelling through Czechoslovakia might have survived.

Our train reached Germany after a trip that lasted more than ten days. The one stop that I remember most vividly was a freight station in Berlin. Here, I believe, we remained for only a few hours before going on to Oranienburg, some forty kilometres away, where the concentration camp of Sachsenhausen, our final destination, was located. I had two experiences at that station in Berlin that I have never forgotten. Shortly after the train had come to a halt I heard a German woman exclaim for all to hear: 'Es stinkt schon wieder von Juden!' ('It stinks of Jews again.') About an hour later our new SS guard – they changed guards every few days – climbed off the train and got himself a cup of coffee. He must have seen me looking longingly at his cup. Without a word, he handed me the coffee and got himself another cup. This was my first warm drink since we left Gliwice.

Beyond being able to attribute the German woman's outburst to a deep-seated hatred of Jews and acknowledging the action of the SS guard as an unexpected act of humanity, I have never been able to reconcile these two events to my own satisfaction, other than to end up with the trite conclusion that generalisations about the Holocaust, about German guilt or about what Germans knew or did not know, do not help us understand the forces that produced one of the world's greatest tragedies. Nor do they help explain what it is in human nature that enables human beings to plan and commit the genocides and the many other mass murders to which mankind has been subjected during my own lifetime. Of course, even less do they answer the question of how, in the midst of all these terrible events, some people find the strength and moral courage to oppose or, at the very least, not commit these monstrous crimes that others perpetrate with ease.

We arrived in Oranienburg not long after leaving Berlin. Instead of going directly to Sachsenhausen, we ended up at the Heinkel aircraft factory. We spent about two weeks there, supposedly in quarantine; at least that is what we were told. Here Michael, Janek and I, together with others from our transport, were housed in a large hangar. The hangar was warm and even though we slept on the ground, it was a relief finally to be inside with a roof over our heads. My feet had already begun to hurt on the train, but because of the cold and snow I had been afraid to take off my shoes there. Now, in the hangar, I removed them for the first time since leaving Auschwitz and noticed that my feet were swollen and discoloured. But I did not let that worry me since I convinced myself that after a few days in a warm place everything would be fine again.

Our rather comfortable life at the Heinkel factory came to an end sooner than I would have liked. One morning we were ordered to proceed on foot to Sachsenhausen. Michael and

Janek were with me, together with other men from our Auschwitz transport. It was becoming increasingly difficult for me to
walk, but my two friends helped me along. In order to get from
Heinkel to Sachsenhausen, which was not all that far, we had
to walk through Oranienburg. Here the German townspeople
stared at us or turned their backs as we passed. Along the way
some children threw stones at us. I was relieved when I finally
saw the entrance to the concentration camp of Sachsenhausen
with its inscription ARBEIT MACHT FREI (Work makes you free).

This slogan, so surreal given its context, was no more
bizarre than the policies that brought us to Sachsenhausen. In
January 1945 Germany was fighting for its survival and yet the
Nazi regime was willing to use its rapidly dwindling resources –
rail facilities, fuel and troops – to move half-starved and dying
prisoners from Poland to Germany. Was it to keep us from falling into the hands of the Allies or to maintain Germany's supply of slave labour? The insanity of it all is hard to fathom,
unless one thinks of it as a game concocted by the inmates of
an asylum for the criminally insane.

*Chapter 6*

# Liberation

The barracks in Sachsenhausen were arranged in a semi-circle along the periphery of the *Appellplatz* (exercise grounds) – all within the range of machine guns mounted on the balcony of the SS administrative building and the guard towers along the camp's wall. From the *Appellplatz* one could see inscriptions with slogans proclaiming: REDEN IST SILBER, SCHWEIGEN IST GOLD (Talk is silver, silence is gold) and FREIHEIT DURCH ARBEIT (Freedom through work), as well as ARBEIT MACHT FREI, painted in big white letters over the dirty walls of the barracks. In the middle of the *Appellplatz* stood a structure that resembled a village well. It was the camp gong or bell. Every morning it summoned the inmates to the *Appellplatz* where they were to be counted. The roll call meant hours and hours of waiting for the counting to end.

For those of us in the *Revier* (infirmary), where I ended up not long after arriving in Sachsenhausen, the gong did not mean standing in line for hours. Here the orderly would simply call out our names and, if there was no answer, he would walk over to the bed from which he expected a reply, throw a fast glance at the person lying there, cross out the name and continue counting. This short interruption in the counting process rarely produced any expressions of grief on the part of the other patients. It had become routine, a non-event.

As soon as I arrived in Sachsenhausen I was forced to accept that my feet were severely frostbitten. I had tried for a week or more to avoid going to the infirmary, although the toes on my right foot were getting blacker by the day. Those on the left foot were also rather discoloured, but not so badly. I was afraid to go to the infirmary because I knew from past experience in Auschwitz that the surest way to end up in the gas chambers was to enter the sick ward of a camp. But my pain kept getting worse, and Michael and Janek – we stayed together after we arrived in Sachsenhausen – kept telling me that I had nothing to lose by having a doctor look at my toes. They finally convinced me and helped get me to the infirmary. On the way I kept telling them that all I needed was some cream or other medication, and my feet would be fine. I was certainly not going to stay in the hospital and let them kill me after they cured me, which was as likely to happen in Sachsenhausen as it was in Auschwitz.

When I arrived at the hospital I was told to take off my shoes. A person in a white coat, who seemed to be in charge, took a quick look at my feet and told me to lie down on a big wooden table. Then he stepped out of the room and soon returned with some other men. Before I knew what was happening, two of them appeared on either side of the table. As if on command, they grabbed my arms and legs and held me down. I started to scream, but a white towel or gauze was placed over my face and I could feel a fluid with a very strong odour being poured over it – it was ether, I learned later. I was out almost immediately. When I woke up I was in a hospital ward in a single bed. As soon as I realised that the lower parts of both my legs were heavily bandaged I became terribly scared. 'They amputated my feet!' I sobbed. That, I knew, meant death once the SS guards embarked on their next regular hospital selection, looking for the sickest inmates to kill.

I asked one of the orderlies what had been done to me and he said that two of my toes had been amputated. I did not believe him and decided to see for myself. Although at that point I really did not feel anything because the anaesthesia had not yet worn off entirely, I started to complain of terrible pain. I continued to cry until a doctor came. After asking me some questions he began to take off my bandages. That really hurt, but I was not going to stop him: I had to know whether I still had my feet. When I saw that they had not been amputated, and even though I could not really make out how many of my toes were gone, I relaxed, utterly exhausted and in ever more pain.

Although the doctors had amputated only two of my toes, the others on both feet had also been frostbitten, though much less severely. Over the next few weeks they worked very hard to save those that remained. In the meantime I was slowly recovering from the operation. At first I walked on crutches but soon managed to move about with the aid of a cane or a single crutch. I considered that quite an achievement because I had been terribly worried that I would never walk again. Now I began to believe that the doctors and nurses were telling the truth when they assured me that my toes would grow back. 'After all,' they would say, 'don't you remember when you were little, that your teeth fell out and you got new ones?' 'Yes,' I replied, 'that is true.' 'It's the same with toes – if they are cut off only once before you are twenty-one, they will grow back, just like your teeth.'

Not long after my operation, a man who had been visiting another patient stopped by my bed. He wanted to know my name, where I had been before I ended up in the infirmary and whether my foot still hurt. He told me that he came from Norway, that his name was Odd Nansen and that one of his friends, also from Norway, was in a nearby bunk in my ward. Mr Nansen returned a few days later with cookies, a picture book with big letters and a pencil. 'You need to learn to read and write, and to draw pictures,' he said. Thereafter, whenever he came to visit, he brought me something to eat, usually sweets, which I had not seen or tasted in years, and he always wanted to know what progress I had made with my writing. I later learned that the Norwegian and Danish inmates of the camp received food packages from the Swedish Red Cross, which they frequently shared with other prisoners. Every so often Mr Nansen would also speak with the ward's orderly, hand him something (usually tobacco or cigarettes) and tell him to take good care of me. Soon I came to look forward to Mr Nansen's visits, not only because he always brought me something nice, but because we talked about many things, especially about what we would do once the war was over. He sounded very much like my father when he kept saying that the Germans would soon lose the war, that I would then go to school with other children, learn to read and write and be reunited with my parents. Mr Nansen also spoke frequently of his wife and children in Norway. He expected to see them as soon as we were liberated and promised that I would get a chance to meet them.

The barrack that housed my ward in the infirmary was constructed of wood, like most of the other barracks in the camp. It had a few little windows and one or two round ventilation holes cut out of the ceiling, which I noticed only after they were forced open one day. Since I had arrived in the infirmary I had heard more and more Allied aircraft flying over the camp at night as well as during the day. They were on their way to bomb Berlin. After a while, as the flights overhead increased and more bombs fell on Oranienburg, the Allies began to drop flares around the camp's perimeter to ensure that no bombs would be directed there. The sound of the bombing was terrifying, though, and made our barrack shake, but we felt safe, knowing that they were trying to protect us. Then one day, as the planes were again flying over, there was a tremendous explosion that shook our barrack more violently than usual, followed by an even louder scream from one of the beds. 'They hit me, they killed me, the bastards!' I heard a man scream. Everyone who could sit up, did so. Then we all burst out laughing as if on command. One of the covers of the ventilation holes had been forced loose by the explosion and had fallen on the man. When he realised that it was not a bomb and that he was still alive, even he could not resist laughing. I don't remember ever laughing either in Auschwitz or Sachsenhausen until then. This first occasion brought us some welcome comic relief, although, given where we were, there was something macabre about the laughter resounding around the room.

It slowly dawned on our SS guards that the camp was the only place that could provide a safe haven from Allied bombing raids. Soon we heard that many of them would bring their families into the camp whenever the air-raid sirens sounded in Oranienburg. Oh, how we relished this information and how it must have irked them. To think that the Germans now finally feared for their lives and had to seek protection in our camp! That made us feel good, even though one or two stray bombs did fall just inside the camp wall and killed a few inmates.

At regular intervals a loudspeaker in our ward broadcast Nazi propaganda news. We had developed a special system for listening to it. For example, whenever they reported that five German fighter planes had shot down thirty Allied bombers and their fighter escorts, we assumed the opposite to be true. News from the western or eastern front was treated by us in the same way. Then, one day, a special news item caught our attention: 'The Jew Roosevelt, President of America, has died!' the announcer gleefully repeated a number of times. Of course, we assumed that Hitler had died and started to congratulate each other. This time, unfortunately, it was not Hitler but Roosevelt who had in fact died.

I don't remember whether it was before or after President Roosevelt's death that Mr Nansen came to see me for the last time. He looked very troubled as he told me that he and the other Norwegians would be leaving the camp within the next few days to be taken to safety in Sweden. He said that he had tried everything to be allowed to take me along, but it was unfortunately not possible. In any event, we would all be free soon and meet again after the war. He gave me a strong handshake, wrote down his name and address on a piece of paper and told me to take good care of myself. I was very sad after he left and wondered whether I would ever see Mr Nansen again. Much later I realised that Mr Nansen had probably saved my life by periodically bribing the orderly in charge of our barrack with cigarettes or tobacco to keep my name off the list of 'terminally ill' patients, which the SS guards demanded every few weeks 'to make room for other inmates'.

Not long after Mr Nansen left I woke up one morning to the usual sound of the camp gong. The sun was not shining and it promised to be a rainy day. I remembered that the bandages on my foot would have to be changed again. This was always very painful because too much skin had been cut off around the amputated big toe, leaving an exposed bone over which the doctor, every few days, tried to pull the skin. The thought occurred to me that it would be wonderful if I woke up one morning and found that my toes had begun to grow again or, at least, if I could find some excuse for not having the wound re-bandaged. Then the orderly came into the room, flustered and without his usual list. Rushing through the ward, he announced that Sachsenhausen was being evacuated. Everybody able to walk had to get out of bed and line up on the *Appellplatz*.

The barrack was suddenly very quiet. The silence was interrupted only by the closing of the door as the orderly left the ward. There were people with me in this big drab room whose legs had been amputated and others who were in body casts. Others still were in the last throes of some terrible disease. Certainly none of these individuals could leave. I decided that I could make it and started to get dressed. So did a few others in the room. They must have been thinking what I was thinking, and that made all of us hurry. Camp evacuation meant long marches and overcrowded trains, like those that had brought me to Sachsenhausen. But it also meant that people who could not walk would be shot wherever they were found – on the roadside or in their beds. I imagined the SS guards with their big boots walking from bed to bed in the infirmary, shooting everyone left behind.

I found my cane and a piece of bread and limped out of the room, leaving behind the moans of those who could not get out of their beds. In the small hospital yard, separated from the other barracks by a wire fence, people were hurrying towards the gate leading to the *Appellplatz*. As I followed them, I suddenly realised how fast I was walking. My foot did not seem to hurt. I only hoped that the SS would not notice me with my cane. I knew that I had to be evacuated with the camp's other inmates if I wanted to stay alive.

When I reached the *Appellplatz* I started to look for Janek and Michael. They were nowhere to be seen. I wondered whether they had been shipped to another camp, for they had visited me only once, shortly after my operation. Hundreds of people were standing around on the *Appellplatz* with blankets over their shoulders and pots or canteens in their hands. The SS guards were in full combat dress. They appeared nervous and the dogs that were their constant companions barked much of the time. I managed to walk unnoticed to a spot near the rear of a column. Now a long wait began. Many hours passed. Rain started to fall, making standing difficult. I ate the piece of bread I had saved from the day before. The nerves in my right foot began to twitch, giving me the sensation that the amputated toes were still there. I could feel them wiggle and pressed my left shoe on my right to stop it. That did not really help much. I was very tired and finally sat down.

After what seemed a long, long wait, the first column started to move out through the main gate under the administrative building. I noticed a group of five men with blankets and rucksacks on their backs. They stood close to where I was sitting.

One of them was a doctor I knew from the hospital who had always been very kind to me. I limped over to him and he greeted me with a smile. 'Doctor, may I march with you?' I asked. 'Yes, of course,' he said, looking at my cane and the oversized shoes I was wearing, given to me in the hospital. 'We are going to try to leave with the second transport tomorrow morning. Half of the camp is leaving today and the others tomorrow. You should go back to the hospital and get a good rest.' 'But, Doctor, are you also going back to the hospital?' I asked. 'I don't want to stay behind.' He assured me that he was and told me to join him and his friends as they walked back to the infirmary. On the way, the doctor asked me whether my foot hurt. I lied and told him that it did not. I was afraid to tell him the truth because I feared that he would not want to take me along if he thought that I could not make it.

During our walk back the doctor and his friends told me that the front was getting closer and that the Soviet troops were nearing Sachsenhausen and Berlin, and that we would soon be liberated. I had heard similar talk before the evacuation of Auschwitz. People said that you could hear the sound of artillery from the approaching front if you put your ear to the ground, and that the war would soon be over. That was in January 1945, and now it was already April and I was in yet another camp. That explains why I was not particularly excited about all this talk of our impending liberation. Besides, I could never quite believe that there would actually come a time when the war would be over and I would be free and able to go to school.

Once, when Mr Nansen told me that after the war I would learn to read and write in a school with many other children, I remember wondering whether school would be like a big concentration camp for children, but where there would be lots of food and I would never be hungry again.

When we reached the infirmary the doctor told me to go to my ward and get a good night's sleep. As I opened the door of the ward I could sense fear gripping the patients who had stayed behind. They must have expected the SS with their dogs and guns. There was a general sigh of relief when they saw it was only me. I was swamped with questions and reported what I had heard: that the Russians were coming closer, that there would be another transport tomorrow, and that there was nothing to worry about tonight. Then I went to sleep with my clothes and shoes on in order to be ready next morning.

The sun was shining through the small windows of our ward when I woke up. I jumped out of bed as fast as I could and hurried over to where the doctor had his quarters. The door was open but nobody was inside. Everything pointed to a sudden departure. There were empty cans, paper and rags on the floor and on the straw mattresses of the beds. As I hobbled through the room I called out the doctor's name. There was no answer. Fear choked my throat as I realised what had happened. 'The doctor left me behind!' I limped out of the room into the hospital yard and through the gate. The *Appellplatz* was deserted! But I remembered the machine guns on the balcony of the administrative building and on the guardhouses.

Without looking up at them, I limped back to the barrack as fast as I could, trying to stay close to the wall in order not to be seen by the SS guards behind those guns.

'He left me behind!' I cried, throwing myself on the floor next to the bed of Marek, my Polish neighbour whose legs were in a cast. Marek must have been in his mid-twenties. Except for me, he was the youngest person in the ward. We had become friends as soon as he had arrived at the infirmary. 'Why didn't you tell me? Why didn't you wake me up? I don't want to die with you, I don't want to die!' He pulled me up to his bed and, with tears in his eyes, told me that the last group had left either late at night or early in the morning. I don't know how long I had been sitting on his bed when I heard him whisper, as if talking to himself, 'They were going to take my casts off next week. Now they'll bury me with them.' I limped over to my bed. My feet hurt. Moans and muffled cries filled the room. This is it, I thought.

A little while later I heard Marek say, 'You can walk. Why don't you leave the hospital and hide someplace in an empty barrack?' This possibility had not occurred to me, not even when I realised that the doctor and his friends had deserted me. Had I thought of it, I probably would have done so. Now, as I lay in my bed with my clothes on and the cane by my side, I did not want to hide any more. I had lost the desire to live and the fear of dying. It was a wonderful feeling, complete emptiness. My feet seemed no longer to hurt; I was not hungry any more. 'I hope they come soon,' I thought as I remembered having had a similar sensation in Auschwitz when, with no hope of escape, I waited for the truck that was to take me to the gas chamber.

Hours passed and I was still alive. The pounding of heavy artillery made our barrack tremble. Some people were sitting up in their beds looking at their neighbours, as if to reassure themselves that they were still alive. In between the heavy bombardment, we could hear machine-gun fire. 'They must be fighting in Oranienburg already. Somebody should go and see what is happening.' Marek turned to me: 'You can walk,' he said. 'Go and find out.' I slid down from the bed, limped out of the ward and began to crawl along the outer wall of the barracks through the hospital yard to the gate. The *Appellplatz* was still deserted. Not far away from me something fell to the ground. It looked like a piece of metal. Heavy machine-gun fire could be heard coming from different places outside the camp's wall. I looked up at the balcony of the administrative building. There was nobody behind the big gun. I walked a few steps further until I could see another watchtower along the wall of the camp. It, too, was empty. I limped back to the ward as fast as I could, stormed through the door and screamed, 'They are gone, they are gone! The SS has run away! The machine-gun towers are empty!'

Very excited, I reported what I had seen. Nobody seemed to believe me because Marek called me over to his bed and asked whether I might not have been mistaken. Once more I recounted what I had seen. 'Those metal pieces are probably shrapnel,' he said. 'When you're outside, try to stay under the overhang of the barrack.' He suggested that I rest my feet for a while before going out again.

A little later I was at my position near the hospital fence once more. I stayed there for quite some time. The shooting came closer and closer. Then, all of a sudden, I heard a squeaking noise and realised that the big gate under the camp's administrative building was being opened. I hid behind a fencepost in fear that the SS was returning. When I looked up again, I saw some soldiers get out of a military vehicle and walk towards the centre of the *Appellplatz* in the direction of the big gong. They did not look like the SS and wore uniforms I had never seen before. But I was still afraid to move. Then I heard the sound of the camp's gong. One of the soldiers was striking it as hard as he could, while another was yelling, '*Hitler kaputt, Hitler kaputt!*' They threw their caps in the air and performed what looked like a wild dance.

First one and then two inmates ventured out very carefully from the barracks in which they were hiding. Others followed. Fearing that the SS had tricked them into believing that the soldiers were Russians, I waited to see when they would lower their guns and start shooting the prisoners. That did not happen. Instead, the soldiers embraced the first few men who reached them and seemed to be giving them cigarettes. By the time I got to the gong, a small group of inmates had surrounded the soldiers, who kept repeating that Hitler was '*kaputt*' and that we had been liberated. More people came out of their hiding places in various barracks. Again I looked all around, hoping to spot Janek and Michael, but they were nowhere to be seen. In fact, I never saw them again and never learned what had happened to them.

The Soviet soldiers who first entered Sachsenhausen had told us that we were free, that we had been liberated. I could not quite grasp what that meant. I had never really thought of liberation as such. My sole concern had been to survive from one day to the next. True, sometimes when lying in my bunk in the infirmary, listening to the sound of British and American bombers flying towards Berlin, I would fantasise that one of these large planes would swoop down, lower a big hook, pick up the entire barrack and take it, with me in it, to England or America. That is something I could imagine, but not liberation.

After the Russians had left, all of us who had greeted them around the camp gong started for the SS kitchen. I followed very slowly, some fifteen or twenty yards behind, and always ready to take cover. I still could not believe that this supposed liberation was real and not some sort of trick concocted by the SS. 'They probably staged this liberation,' I said to myself, 'in order to draw us out of our hiding places.' That is why I did not walk into the kitchen with the rest of the men, but kept my distance. When nothing bad happened, I slowly entered the building and, on my way to the kitchen, noticed an open door to what looked like an office. After making sure that no one was inside, I stepped in and looked around. Above the desk hung a photograph of Hitler; the walls were lined with filing cabinets; a telephone stood on the desk. I looked out of the window and saw a number of men coming out of the kitchen carrying bread and some tin cans.

*Maybe we really have been liberated*, I thought as I climbed on the desk and pulled down Hitler's picture. I threw it on the floor, shattering the frame and the glass. I spat on it and stepped on his face so hard that my feet began to hurt, but still I went on until the picture was torn to pieces. Then I pulled out all the drawers from the filing cabinets and let the files fall to the floor. My work completed, I sat down behind the desk in the soft leather chair and picked up the telephone receiver. The line was dead, but I spoke into it anyway, telling my imagined listeners that Hitler and all Germans were dead. Then I pulled the cord out of the wall and limped over to the kitchen.

There the men were eating everything they could find. Some of them were hanging over big kettles, slurping what looked like soup the SS had left behind. The door to the storeroom was open and a number of men came out carrying armloads of bread and sausages. Everybody was chewing on something. I found two loaves of bread, some onions and a pickle. I began to eat the pickle, which was the only food I had an urge to eat at that moment and which tasted delicious, and limped out of the kitchen to share my 'liberated' food with Marek in the infirmary. People were running back and forth between the barracks and the kitchen – eating all the time while carrying more food. On my way out a man pushed me and snatched one of my loaves of bread, but I was too excited to worry about it.

The news of our liberation had already reached the infirmary by the time I got there. Somebody had brought pails of soup and other food. Marek tried to tell everybody not to eat too much all at once because, being undernourished, they might die from overeating. But no one paid attention. Marek and I split the bread and onions and a remaining piece of the pickle.

In the late afternoon a Russian officer came into our barrack. He told us that all sick people would be cared for by Russian doctors and nurses who were to arrive in a few days. Those who could walk were free to leave the next day. Marek called me over to his bed after the Russian had left. 'We had better try to get out of here on our own,' he said. 'Who knows when the Russians will come and take us to a hospital. Besides, the Germans might retake the camp and we don't want to be here when that happens. You'll have to help me get out of my casts.' He produced a knife and I started to cut. 'Let's leave tomorrow morning, all right?' I agreed, although I would have loved to have been taken to a Russian hospital on a Red Cross truck as the officer had promised.

When I woke up early in the morning, Marek was already practising walking. 'What a day!' he said, pointing to the window. 'The sun is shining, celebrating our liberation,' he exclaimed, and continued, 'I had already given up all hope of ever again seeing my folks in Poland. What a surprise it will be!' and he performed an awkward jig. 'Get ready,' he said to me, 'you are coming to Poland with me and then we'll start looking for your parents.' Yes, my parents. How I wanted to be together with them again! I did not know where my parents were, nor where or how we would be reunited. But even though I had seen many people die in the camps, it never occurred to me that they might not be alive. I was sure that they would find me as soon as they were liberated.

Chapter 7

# Into the Polish Army

The big Sachsenhausen gate was open. Marek and I walked through it, under the administrative building with its tower and the now empty machine-gun nest near the area where some of the SS guards had been housed, and left the camp. We did not look back, either because we were afraid that some guards would suddenly give chase or because we did not want to be reminded of what lay behind us, or both.

It took us a while to reach what looked like a major highway. It was teeming with tanks, military trucks and horse-drawn wagons, carrying men and supplies. The men were waving to us and shouting. 'Polish soldiers,' Marek said, and we waved back, calling out to them in Polish. They threw us loaves of bread as they drove past, chanting anti-Nazi slogans and singing 'Long live Poland!'

We had been told to march away from the front, which was moving closer and closer to Berlin. That meant that we had to go in the direction from which the soldiers were coming.

Along the way we met inmates from other camps. There was much waving and cheering, with everybody wanting to know what camp we came from. For a while the road resembled a street carnival. A Polish military truck offered us a ride to a nearby German town. 'Most of the houses here are empty,' the driver told us, 'the Germans ran away because they are afraid of the Russians.' Then, acting as though he owned the town, he added, 'Move into any of these houses and take anything you find there, compliments of the Polish Kosciuszko Division.' The soldier laughed and drove away. As we walked down one of the streets we met three Jewish girls from Hungary and two young men who had also just been liberated. They asked Marek and me to join them in the search for a house.

It did not take us long to come upon a large two-storey brick house with a garden in front and a large back yard. It must have been abandoned on very short notice because the kitchen table was set and there was even some food still on the plates. 'Let's continue the dinner,' one of the girls suggested. The cellar was stocked with canned fruit, vegetables and even canned meat. We carried some of it up and the girls started a fire and began to cook. What a wonderful dinner it was! My first real meal in years. The trouble was that while it all looked marvellous to me, I could barely swallow more than a few bites. Marek said that my stomach must have shrunk during all those years of near starvation. I did not know whether he was right; all I knew was that I could eat very, very little. Rather than stay at the table, I remembered the chickens and rabbits in the back yard and

that it had taken some persuasion on my part to save the rabbits from our eager cooks. I went out of the house to feed and
play with them. I had found some new furry friends and was
not going to let them be eaten.

Wealthy people must have lived in the house, I thought. It
had many rooms with fine furniture and paintings on the walls.
It was hard for me to imagine, after Kielce, Auschwitz and
Sachsenhausen, that such homes existed and that families
lived in them. The closets were filled with clothing. There were
sheets and towels in drawers, as well as blankets and pillows.
What would I not have given to have my parents with me in this
house!

To the delight of the Hungarian girls, we found a sewing
machine and one of them immediately sat down to make herself a blouse with some material she had found. The men took
all the clothing out of the closets and began to try on suits and
shirts. I found a pair of trousers and, since they were much too
long on me, I simply shortened them with a kitchen knife and
found a string to use as a belt. When I was all done I threw my
prison garb through the open window into the garden. Then I
washed myself. 'No more prisoner,' I thought, but then realised that the water and soap could not rid me of the one thing
that would serve forever as a reminder of the concentration
camp: the blue tattoo with my Auschwitz number on the inside
of my left arm. Carefully, I dried my arm. *Papa will be proud of
me*, I thought. Addressing him, as if reporting for duty, I called
out, 'B-2930 has survived Auschwitz, Sachsenhausen, the

Ghetto of Kielce and Germany! We won, as you predicted we would.'

I enjoyed myself immensely in 'our' beautiful house. It was very comfortable; I had a clean bed all to myself with white sheets, pillows and a quilt cover. It reminded me of Zilina, of our apartment there, and the cosy bed I had in the Grand Hotel. Through the windows of our new house I could see Soviet tanks and trucks and soldiers, all moving towards Berlin. One day, while playing in the street, I noticed a Russian coming out of a nearby house. He was pushing a bicycle. *Oh, to have a bike!* I thought and wondered whether I could still ride one. After all, I had not done so since I'd first learned to ride one in the Henryków factory in Kielce. Now I enviously watched the Russian soldier. As soon as he reached the street he jumped clumsily on the bicycle and immediately fell off. He picked himself up and tried again and again. He started to swear, but the bicycle was unimpressed. I began to laugh. 'Should I show you how it is done?' I asked in Polish, as I helped him pick up the bike. But he continued to swear. Finally, after yet another try, he threw the bike down and proceeded to kick it. 'Don't break it, don't break it!' I cried, pulling on his uniform. He looked at me, spat on the ground and walked away. That is how I became the proud owner of a bike. Of course, I jumped on it immediately and found, to my delight, that I had not forgotten how to ride.

The evenings in our house were lots of fun. Polish officers and soldiers dropped in and brought us food and sweets. They asked about life in the concentration camps, wanted to know where we had been, told us about fighting the Germans, and where they were during the war. Marek and I served as interpreters. They spoke of the conquest of Warsaw, the battles along the Vistula and Oder rivers and the imminent German capitulation. Every evening more and more of them came. They told us about their regiments and they showed me their decorations. One day a new group of soldiers came to visit us. They spoke with Marek and the Hungarian girls, while I was occupied polishing my bike, which I had carried into the house. The conversation dealt with Berlin and the prospects of victory. When Marek left the room to get some water glasses for the vodka they had brought along, the soldiers tried to communicate with the girls, but the girls did not understand Polish. I put my bike aside and asked them whether I could translate for them. 'The girls understand German and I speak Polish,' I said.

Immediately, I became the centre of attention. 'A Polish boy!' they exclaimed, and before I had a chance to explain that I was not a Pole, Marek entered the room. 'Yes, he is Polish,' Marek said. 'He was born in Kielce and now I am taking him back.' He winked at me. 'Let's take him to Poland,' one of the soldiers said. 'He can come with us,' added another. 'I am staying with Marek,' I threw in, and went back to polish my bike. When they had left, Marek came over to me and explained that it might not be such a bad idea to go with the soldiers. After all, they could take care of me better than he could and get me back to Poland faster. There I would soon find my parents. I was not at all persuaded and did not want to lose the only real friend I had.

Early the next morning two soldiers came to visit. One of them had been our guest the night before; the other was an officer. They had brought some chocolate and a bicycle bell. The officer introduced himself and told me that he had heard about me. 'We are with the heavy artillery,' he said, 'and if you come with us, you'll have a great life.' 'Yes,' the soldier chipped in, 'you'll ride in military cars. What a life! No more walking.' 'He's right,' said the officer, 'you'll have all the chocolate you want and we'll let you shoot the cannons.' They talked and talked. Finally, in order not to seem impolite, I promised to think about it. Then I went out and attached the bell to my bike.

We had visitors again in the afternoon. Among the soldiers who came I recognised the two who had dropped by earlier. They came into the garden and played with me. They showed me all kinds of tricks I could do with my bike. One of them asked me whether I wanted to learn how to shoot a gun. He found an old can in the yard, took his pistol out, threw the can into the air and fired. It was a perfect hit. Then he gave me the gun, placed the can on the fence and showed me how to aim. I was having a wonderful time. Another of the soldiers gave me a penknife. Again, they began to speak to me about returning with them to Poland. This time, somewhat to my own surprise, I agreed. Suddenly it all seemed very exciting.

The soldiers picked me up the next morning. Parting from Marek was not easy, but he assured me that I was doing the right thing, and I wanted to believe him. I never saw or heard from him again. My bicycle was loaded on the jeep and, while my friends waved, we drove off. The car sped through the streets of that little German town which had become our temporary home. The jeep stopped in front of a large crowded yard. 'Here we are,' said the driver. 'This is the famous Scout Company of the First Kosciuszko Division.' The yard was full of soldiers, trucks, armoured cars and horses. 'Let's introduce him to the captain,' said one of the soldiers who was holding my bike. We walked into one of the houses. The captain was a tall, heavyset man whom I liked immediately. 'This is Tomek,' reported the driver. 'Yes, yes,' muttered the captain, 'heard a lot about you.' Picking me up in his arms, he immediately made me feel welcome. He then turned to one of the men and ordered him to get the company tailor and shoemaker. 'We'll make a real soldier out of you,' he said to me as he set me down again.

Within a day or two I received something that looked like a Polish uniform, a belt and a pair of shoes. Nothing seemed to be missing. The uniform had military buttons and even a corporal's insignia. 'If you make a good soldier,' the company tailor told me, 'the captain will promote you to sergeant.' I had become a full-fledged soldier, albeit in miniature: the mascot of the Polish army. I don't know exactly what date it was, although it must have been the end of April 1945. I was about two weeks short of my eleventh birthday.

*Thomas in a tailor-made uniform of the Polish Army in 1945, with the soldier who took him to the Jewish orphanage*

At first the tailor and shoemaker, who had made my uniform and shoes, were the soldiers I was closest to in the Scout Company. We ate all our meals together and they soon noticed that I ate very little. That worried them and they decided that they had to find a cure for my lack of appetite. When it appeared that the remedies they had come up with did not work, the shoemaker had an idea. 'Why not try vodka?' he suggested. And out came the bottle. First a spoonful, then two and finally half a *kieliszek* (tumbler), followed by little pieces of bacon. It worked like a charm: within days, I began to eat normally. This cure had the further consequence that, after a while, I could hold my vodka as well as many a soldier. I retained this capacity for vodka until my college days, when friends who had just seen the *Brothers Karamazov* movie, bet me fifteen dollars – a lot of money in those days – that I could not drink a fifth of vodka, as one of the brothers had done in the movie, and jump over a chair. I won the wager, but got so sick afterwards that it was years before I could so much as look at a bottle of vodka again.

Besides showing me how to drink vodka and helping to revive my appetite, the tailor and shoemaker also tried to teach me their trades. I was particularly drawn to what the shoemaker called the 'art of shoemaking', from the stretching, cutting and stitching of the leather to the nailing down of the soles with wooden nails. My new friend was a master at it and as I watched him I thought that it would be fun to become a shoemaker. I still remember all the steps that went into the production of an entirely hand-made pair of shoes.

Some days after I joined it, the Scout Company received orders to move on Berlin. Despite the fact that we were probably stationed no more than thirty kilometres from the outskirts of Berlin, our progress was quite slow, since the company was not fully mechanised. While we had some trucks, one or two cars and a few armoured vehicles, our supplies and maybe even the ammunition were transported on horse-drawn wagons, which brought up the rear and slowed down our advance. The roads were also crowded with advancing Soviet troops, whose tanks and artillery pieces kept passing us amid a great deal of shouting and general confusion. It was all very exciting to me, especially as I was permitted to ride in one of the armoured vehicles, although I had to sleep in a horse-drawn wagon.

When we reached Berlin the fighting for the city was still in full swing. Artillery and heavy machine-gun fire could be heard in the distance. Death and destruction were all around us. Most of the buildings along our route had been burned out or reduced to rubble. The houses that were still standing were covered with bullet holes. Bodies of dead German and Soviet soldiers and of civilians were lying in the streets or on the mounds of brick and cement that were all that remained of what had once been private homes, apartment houses or office buildings.

Our destination was a park not far from the Brandenburg Gate. The park was already largely occupied by Soviet troops with their artillery pieces and katyushas, their rocket-propelled field guns. My company established itself in one part of the park, not far from the katyusha batteries, which were making a terrible noise every time they were fired. I still remember one of the soldiers, probably a corporal or sergeant, who was in charge of a katyusha mounted atop a truck, hurling anti-fascist slogans and obscenities in the direction of the German defenders of the city each time he gave the order to release the rockets. Although the Germans seemed no longer to be firing their cannons in our direction, I was told to sleep in the armoured car at night and to stay in or near it during the day, because no one knew how long the Germans would continue to fight.

Besides, there were still many German snipers around. The day after we arrived in Berlin one of our soldiers had been killed by a sniper shooting from a building at one of our trucks that had left the park to reconnoitre some suspected German positions.

As the fighting died down some soldiers decided to go fishing in a nearby pond and took me along. When we got there, one of them threw a hand grenade into the water. Within minutes the surface was covered with dead fish floating belly-up. My friends scooped up some fish in a bucket they had brought along. They called it 'speed fishing'. I don't know what they did with the fish, but if they cooked them, they did not share any with me.

I have only tried to fish a few times in my life and have never had much success at it. Once, on my first fishing outing with my sons, who were then still quite young, I cast my rod with real gusto and, to my great shock and that of my sons, hooked the shirt of a fisherman standing on the other side of the pier. He did not look very happy when he saw what had happened. While I was trying to disentangle my hook from his shirt, my sons, fearing that the fisherman would attack me with the long knife hanging from his belt, kept moving ever further away from me. But as soon as I told the man that I had never fished before he burst out laughing and wished me more success the next time. At that moment I thought of that Berlin pond back in 1945, which had actually been my first fishing experience – but certainly not the type of fishing I would recommend.

The news that Berlin had capitulated reached us a day after the fishing expedition at the pond. Of course, there was great rejoicing throughout our park, with a lot of shots being fired into the air from whatever weapons were handy. At the same time, vodka was being dispensed to the troops. Polish and Soviet soldiers could be seen embracing each other and sharing their liquor and cigarettes. Everybody was singing and dancing. A Polish soldier from our company gave me some swigs from his vodka bottle. The park had turned into a veritable carnival. As it got darker and the festivities gradually died down, I crawled into the armoured car that had been my bed for the past few days and was soon fast asleep. That is how I helped liberate Berlin!

The war itself would not be over for another week or so. My company, together with other units, was ordered to move out in pursuit of German troops that had retreated from Berlin. That day or a day later, we reached the edge of a forest. A whole German division was apparently dug in among the trees. Although they outnumbered us, their commanders were willing to negotiate an orderly surrender. The negotiations continued through much of the night. By morning, what had been expected to be a major surrender operation led only to the capture of the German officers who had taken part in the negotiations. The rest of the German division had simply vanished into thin air. Along the way, though, we would from time to time run into groups of German soldiers who would surrender to us without putting up any resistance. It was quite an exhilarating experience for me to see German officers tremble in fear as they approached us, when only months earlier they had inspired terror in all who stood before them.

A few days later we learned that Germany had surrendered. The celebrations were even wilder than those that took place when we heard that Berlin had capitulated. The shooting and drinking continued for hours on end, into the night and even on to the next day. The soldiers in my company were singing the Polish national anthem and all kinds of other Polish songs I had never heard before. Every so often someone would raise his glass or bottle and drink to Poland and to the victorious Allied armies. Some soldiers stood around in small groups and spoke of home and of their families in Poland; others, with tears in their eyes, kept saying that they never thought they would live to see the end of the war and the defeat of Germany.

I was not sure whether to be happy or sad. Of course, I was happy that the war was over and that we had been liberated. But when the soldiers spoke of their families and of home I was reminded that I did not know where my home was. I had no home without my parents and I did not know where they were. Strangely enough, the thought that they might have died in the camps never crossed my mind. I was sure that if I had survived, they must have survived too, and they would find me! In the meantime, Scout Company was my home. But what would happen to me when all the soldiers left? I decided that there would be time enough to answer that question and, for all I knew, it might never present itself since I was sure my parents would find me before the army was disbanded.

I had a wonderful time as we moved through Germany after its capitulation. Along the way some soldiers from my company had come upon what remained of a German circus. There they found a beautiful pony and a miniature cart. They brought both to me and one of the soldiers told me, 'We liberated it for you. It needed a good Polish home.' I spent many hours combing and feeding my new companion. I would ride the pony for fun, but when the company had to move, I would sit in my little cart and follow the horse-drawn wagons that were carrying our supplies. Along the way, soldiers from other companies would wave and shout to me as we passed. Before I got the pony, I had also acquired a small pistol of the type that women could carry in their handbags. I think it was my shoemaker friend who gave it to me. Since he had warned me that the five bullets in the magazine were the only ammunition he had been able to find for the gun, I shot it only once in order to find out whether it really worked. It did. From then on I carried the pistol very proudly in a holster the shoemaker had made for me, and polished it often.

We moved at a much slower pace through Germany than before its capitulation and stayed for days in different towns. Many of the houses were empty, since their owners had fled in advance of the Soviet troops. We basically had the run of the place. Some of the soldiers from my company amused themselves by breaking windows and causing all kinds of other damage. Encouraging me to follow their example, the soldiers would tell me that the Germans deserved that and more for all the suffering they had caused in Poland.

I did not see much excitement in breaking windows and preferred to play or ride my pony whenever we stopped in a town for a few days. But one day a young soldier invited me to come along with him for some good fun. With his *pepeshka* sub-machine gun slung over his shoulder – this was a gun with a round magazine that almost all the Soviet and Polish soldiers used at the time – he guided me to a narrow street and pointed to the telephone poles lining the road. 'See those white porcelain cups with the electric wires wound around them?' he asked. 'We are going to try to shoot them down,' he said, as he clicked a lever on the gun so that it would shoot only one bullet at a time. He had many misses, but also some hits. When hit, the porcelain would shatter on the street below, adding to the noise the *pepeshka* made. After a while, he handed me the weapon. First he had me aim it at a nearby fence 'to give me a feel for the gun'. It was not very heavy and the round magazine seemed to help steady it. I had no trouble hitting the fence, but it took me a while to hit the targets on the telephone poles. I got the hang of it after a while, though. From then on my friend and I would go hunting for these porcelain cups whenever we came to a new town. To this day, whenever I see telephone poles with their porcelain cups, I recall, not without some shame, my acts of vandalism of long ago, and feel a suppressed yearning to try it at least once more.

Our meandering through Germany came to an end when my company, with all its equipment, was ordered to embark on a train for Poland. The train stopped many times along the way, frequently alongside others crowded with Soviet troops. We would then all get off our trains and engage in friendly banter. Poles and Russians would trade in all types of 'liberated' items. The Russians would display their czassy (watches) – they would proudly show off four or five watches on each arm – and offer to trade some of them for other watches or jewellery. They seemed fascinated by what made watches tick. I remember one of them putting a watch under the wheel of a railroad car while the train was being shunted about, just to see what would happen. Everybody cheered when he retrieved the flattened timepiece and ceremoniously displayed the shattered workings to his audience.

There were more cheers and much rejoicing when the train crossed into Poland. Our destination was a military garrison in the Polish city of Siedlice. There I shared quarters with a group of men from my company. The soldiers played a lot of soccer and cards as they waited to be demobilised and allowed to return to private life. There was also a lot of horseplay. One popular pastime was to wait for some unsuspecting soldier to enter one of the portable outdoor privies near the barracks; a few soldiers would then materialise out of nowhere, lift the privy off its hole and tip the wooden structure on its side with the poor victim in it screaming and swearing.

At the garrison in Siedlice I started to spend more and more time with a young soldier in my company who was Jewish. Over the years I have forgotten the names of many people, but the name I most regret not remembering is that of this young soldier, although I still have the photograph he gave me, taken of the two of us together in our uniforms. While I imagine that many of the soldiers in my company guessed that I was Jewish, I kept that information to myself for fear, probably unjustified, that they would no longer treat me as one of their own. I did, however, tell my friend, but asked him not to let the other soldiers know. Whenever we talked, he kept asking me what I planned to do in the future. Of course, I had no idea, had not really thought about it, probably because I expected my parents to find me any day soon. He kept shaking his head, very delicately trying to make me understand that it would take them a long time to find me, assuming that they were alive.

One day he let me know that he had to go away for a few days. He returned from his trip very excited and told me that he had found a wonderful Jewish orphanage in Otwock, near Warsaw. He had told the director about me and she indicated that I would be most welcome to stay there until I found my parents. I would love it there, my friend assured me; I would meet many children my age who had also survived the war. Besides, our company commander had told him that a military garrison was not really the right place for an eleven-year-old boy.

A few days later, my friend and I were on a train bound for Otwock.

*Chapter 8*

# Waiting to Be Found

The Jewish orphanage on the outskirts of Otwock was housed in a longish, rectangular two-storey white building with a big front yard and a garden in the back. Surrounding it all was a thick pine forest where mushrooms, blueberries and wild strawberries grew in abundance. A narrow paved road led to the orphanage from the town. The orphanage could also be reached by walking through the forest along some well-trodden paths. Before the Second World War, Otwock was a well-known resort where people suffering from tuberculosis would stay at its many sanitariums. Some of these facilities, converted to other uses during the war, lined one side of the road leading to the orphanage.

For me the Jewish orphanage served as a halfway house between one life and another. It was here that I underwent a gradual transformation from a perennially frightened and hungry camp inmate, struggling to survive, to a relatively normal eleven-year-old child. I enjoyed almost every minute of my stay at the orphanage, although there were moments when I looked back with nostalgia on the adventure-filled life I had enjoyed in the Polish army and wished I still had my pony with me.

The orphanage housed teenage boys and girls, as well as some younger children, separated into groups. I was placed with the oldest group of boys. Here I was the youngest of its fifteen to twenty members, which made me feel very important. Not all the children in the orphanage were real orphans. Some still had one or both parents and had been placed there temporarily while their mothers and fathers sought to re-establish their lives or were still abroad. I was among those whose parents, as far as we knew, had been killed during the war. We were the real orphans and saw ourselves as the orphanage's tough guys, lording it over the other kids. In some perverse way our attitude resembled that of hardened criminals or 'lifers' in a prison who take pride in their status. At the same time, of course, I secretly continued to believe that my parents were alive and would find me one day soon.

The vast majority of children in the orphanage had been hidden during the war by Polish families or in convents. During that period some of them lived under terribly difficult conditions. One girl, Tamara, who was my age and soon became my best friend, spent more than two years hiding in the low attic of a house. There was no room in that attic for her to walk or even to stand up. By the time she was liberated her legs had become seriously deformed. Other children and their parents had managed to obtain false identity papers. This enabled them to pass themselves off as Poles in various towns and villages around the country, though they lived in constant fear of being denounced to the Germans. Some of these children were left to fend for themselves when their parents were caught in SS raids. Among the older kids there were also some survivors of German work camps. Each of us had a story to tell that was more horrendous than the next, but we rarely, if ever, talked about our past, although my friends loved to hear me regale them with tales of my life in the Polish army.

I was the only one in the orphanage who had survived Auschwitz, and our administrators publicised this fact. As a result I was frequently interviewed by journalists and trotted out to meet important visitors. I even appeared occasionally in the newsreels that were shown in Polish cinemas in those pre-television days. From time to time we were also visited by representatives of the American Joint Distribution Committee (the 'Joint', as it was known), whose organisation was, I believe, the orphanage's main benefactor.

We were treated very well in the orphanage. When I first arrived I was examined by a doctor who decided that I was too thin for my age and needed to be put on a special diet to gain weight. For quite some time thereafter my breakfast, in addition to the standard bread and boiled eggs, consisted of a bowl of light cream into which I usually stirred strawberry jam or orange marmalade. Some kids who were on this special diet did not like the cream we were served. Since I loved it, I frequently traded my eggs for their cream. Never before had I eaten so well! There were moments when, on seeing all that wonderful food in front of me, I felt sure that it was all a dream and that, instead of the white cream I thought I saw, I would wake up and look down on the snow we ate on the Auschwitz death transport. At the end of summer, when the mushrooms in our forest were bursting out of the ground, Cook would send us out to gather them for her. For the next few days we could count on wonderful mushroom soup or some special mushroom dish. I thought I was in heaven.

When I arrived at the orphanage I did not for all practical purposes know how to read or write, apart from what my parents had tried to teach me surreptitiously in Kielce. I am quite sure, though, that I must have received some individual instruction from one of our counsellors before I was sent to the nearby Polish grade school attended by the other kids from the orphanage. Curiously enough, I remember almost nothing about that school, how long I was there, what grade I was in or what I learned. It may well be that I was there for only a brief period. But a couple of things stand out in my mind from my time at that school: the big crucifix that hung above the blackboard and the daily prayer our Polish classmates intoned every morning while crossing themselves. Even though I did not participate in this exercise and was quite uncomfortable just standing there, I soon learned the words by heart and can to this day still recite them in Polish.

I also remember the day I dunked one of Tamara's

braids – she sat in front of me – into the inkpot on my desk. She gave me a terribly nasty look, but said nothing to our Polish teacher. Instead she reported me to the head counsellor when we returned to the orphanage. A few days later I was made to appear before an honours tribunal composed of some older kids. As punishment, the tribunal sentenced me to carry Tamara's books to and from school for a period of two weeks and to perform any other chores she cared to assign to me. That led to our becoming inseparable friends and, after a while, she even volunteered to mend my socks.

Much of our free time in the orphanage was spent playing sports. Despite the amputation of my two toes, I could run very fast and I gradually developed into a good soccer player. Since I could kick equally well with both feet, I was able to play in a number of different positions. As a result I was always among the first to be chosen when the two best players at the orphanage selected their teams. I also learned to play table tennis, which was a big sport there, and after a while could beat many of those who had taught me the game. During my stay the orphanage created a Boy Scout troop. Although we were still waiting for proper uniforms by the time I left, I very much enjoyed the activities we performed as Scouts.

In the evenings, particularly on weekdays and after the Sabbath services, Polish and Jewish books would be read aloud. At times, too, some of the kids would stage musical recitals. I remember that one of the older boys played the piano very well, while others sang or performed on some other musical instrument. I soon learned, to my great regret, that I lacked any musical talent and could not even carry a tune. From time to time some of us older kids would be taken on excursions outside of Otwock or be allowed to travel as a group by ourselves. Once we were given permission to take the train to Warsaw, a mere twenty kilometres from Otwock. The occasion for our trip was the reopening of the main bridge over the Vistula connecting Warsaw and its Praga suburb, which had been destroyed during the war. We had been given money for our tickets and, when we reached the station, somebody suggested that I buy the tickets, since I was the youngest and could claim that we were all too young to pay the full fare. When I got to the ticket window I made myself shorter than I was and got the reduced-price tickets. We spent the extra money on sweets and felt really proud of ourselves.

We grew vegetables in the garden behind the orphanage and, if we wished, could have our own small plot for individual cultivation. We grew cucumbers, carrots, beans, cabbages and tomatoes. I loved working in my little garden, particularly after one of the kids showed me how to change the shape of a cucumber by putting the still-small plant into a bottle. After following his instructions I faithfully inspected my bottled cucumber every morning to see what was happening to it. My experiment did not turn out the way I had hoped because, when I tried to get the ripe but deformed cucumber out of the bottle, I mutilated it instead.

To one side of our building, near the garden, the beekeeper kept a row of beehives. Fascinated by what he was doing, I volunteered to help him one day. He told me what to do and, after donning the protective net he handed me, I tried to operate the bellows used to smoke out the bees in order to enable the beekeeper to remove the honey. As I struggled unsuccessfully to make the bellows work, I began to get stung on my gloveless hands and decided to run, despite the warnings of the beekeeper to stand still. The beehives were about twenty metres from the orphanage building and, as I tried to outrun the bees, whole swarms began to follow me. With my protective net no longer in place I was being stung all over my face and neck. I made it to the building and slammed the door shut, leaving most of the bees behind. The nurse I went to see later said that I was very lucky because, had I been allergic to bee stings, I might well have died. As it was I was in considerable pain for a number of days from my swollen hands, face and neck. I never again went near the beehives.

One day two of my friends found a handgun in the forest and they told me about it because, as they put it, I knew 'how to handle guns'. They had buried the gun in the forest and wanted me to see whether it worked. My friends dug it up and I inspected it with all the apparent expertise I could muster for their benefit. It was quite dirty and even rusty in places, and I had no idea if it would work or not. What to do? Here we faced a real dilemma, since there was only one bullet in the magazine: if we tested the gun we would end up with a weapon but no ammunition; if we decided to save our only bullet, however, we would never know whether the gun worked. Eventually our curiosity got the better of us and we convinced ourselves that at some future time we would be able to acquire the needed ammunition. Since I had bragged to all willing to listen that I had had lots of experience shooting guns, my friends decided that I should be the one to try it out. I was not happy about this decision because I had been told by those who gave me my little gun in the Polish army that a dirty and rusty firearm might explode when used. When it became clear that I had no choice but to demonstrate my expertise, I asked my friends to stand clear as I proceeded to aim the pistol at a big tree a few metres away. I pressed the trigger and the gun went off with a loud bang, emitting a great deal of smoke. But I was still standing, gun in hand and uninjured. We decided to re-bury it after wrapping it in some cloth, planning to come back a few days later with bicycle oil or butter and clean it up. In the meantime, though, Polish government placards appeared all over town calling on the population to turn in all weapons. My two friends and I debated what to do with our buried gun and decided to leave it where it was. It is probably still there.

The mail for the orphanage had to be collected from the post office in Otwock. This chore was usually assigned to one or two of the older kids. They hated it, however, because to get to the post office they had to pass a nearby Catholic orphanage, where the Polish kids would bombard them with stones or try to beat them up while hurling anti-Semitic curses at them. Our kids therefore tried to avoid the Catholic orphanage by taking elaborate detours through the forest, although even then they might sometimes be set upon. Not long after I arrived at the orphanage, it was decided that because I did not look Jewish and could easily pass for a Pole, I should be given the job of picking up the mail. This worked for a while, though the Polish kids soon figured out that I came from the Jewish orphanage, and I was no longer immune to their attacks. Being fast on my feet, I usually managed to outrun them, although I could not escape their anti-Semitic catcalls. The worst part of my job as a mailman, though, was that there never was any mail for me.

During my stay at the orphanage its administration was in the hands of the Jewish Bund, a leftist political organisation which, among other things, believed that Jews should help build a socialist Polish state rather than emigrate to Palestine to help create a Jewish one. Those who ran the orphanage therefore made no effort to encourage emigration to Palestine or to engage in activities preparing us for it. This situation did not go unnoticed by Zionist groups in Poland and prompted one of them – a youth organisation called Hashomer Hatzair – to infiltrate the orphanage in order to secretly promote emigration to Palestine. That is how a young woman by the name of Lola ended up at our orphanage and, by the time I arrived at Otwock, had become either the head counsellor or the counsellor for my group. While I am not sure of her precise title, I do know that I adored her, as did all my friends.

I had already been in the orphanage for some time when Lola invited me to go for a walk with her. As we left the grounds she asked me if I had ever considered going to Palestine or whether I planned to stay in Poland. In fact I had never given the matter any thought as I expected that my parents, whenever I found them, would make such decisions for me. Nevertheless, I had heard my father speak of Palestine and of the need for us Jews to have our own country. With his words in my mind, I told Lola, 'I would love to live in Palestine because there I would not have to worry about being called a dirty Jew or have Polish kids throw stones at me.' 'If you are sure that you really want to live there,' Lola said, 'then I will tell you how, but you must promise to keep it secret ...'

After I promised her that the secret would forever be safe with me, Lola told me that some of the older kids, both girls and boys, had already let her know that they wished to live in Palestine and that she, in turn, would help them get there. She had drawn up a list with the names of these kids and, if I was really sure that I wanted to move to Palestine, she would add my name to the list. Of course, I told her that I was more than sure. Lola then explained how the scheme would work. Starting soon, one kid at a time would sneak out of the orphanage and be picked up by some people from Hashomer Hatzair. Each kid would then be taken to a temporary kibbutz in Poland, where arrangements would be made for him or her to be smuggled out of Poland to Palestine via either Italy or France. This process would be repeated every few weeks.

It all sounded terribly exciting. I immediately volunteered to be among the first to run away. But Lola explained that I had to be the last to leave the orphanage because I was 'famous'. The publicity I had attracted as an Auschwitz survivor meant that my disappearance would most certainly spark an investigation which might jeopardise the entire operation. Still, at least my name was on Lola's list and I would not be left behind. I was thrilled at the prospect of living in Palestine.

Some months passed after that conversation with Lola without my hearing anything more about my 'escape'. Then one morning, when I had given up all hope of ever going to Palestine, the director of the orphanage called me to her office. We were usually asked to see the director only if we were in serious trouble, so I was sure that she had found out about Hashomer Hatzair and Lola's scheme and would interrogate me about it. On my way to her office, I worried about what I would say and decided that I would lie rather than risk revealing Lola's plans, which might get her fired. I certainly did not want to lose Lola.

A big smile greeted me when I entered the director's office. *She is trying to trick me*, I thought, *to get me to talk*. After asking me to sit down, the director began to question me about my parents. Did I remember my mother's name? 'Gerda,' I said. 'What did you call her?' she asked next, and I replied, 'Mutti.' 'Do you know where she was born?' I answered that she was born in Göttingen. There were more questions, some also about my father and when I had last seen my parents, and so on. I answered as best I could, still wondering what this was all about. Then the director asked me whether I would recognise my mother if I saw her. 'Of course!' I said, now utterly confused. 'What is this woman driving at?' I asked myself and was sure that she would eventually get to the real reason for my being in her office.

Instead, the director pointed to a letter on her desk. 'I have great news for you, Tomek: your mother is alive! This is a letter from her.'

As soon as I saw the letter, all the excitement and happiness I felt at the director's news vanished. It was written in Polish, and I knew that my mother could not write Polish. Also, the handwriting was clearly not hers. I knew that right away because, even before I knew how to read properly, my father used to make fun of my mother's handwriting by saying that it looked as if a chicken had walked over a piece of paper after stepping into a pot of ink. The letter the director handed me had not been written by my mother.

I felt like crying, but did not want to let the director see how disappointed I was. I told her that the letter did not come from my mother and that it was probably written by someone who wanted to adopt me by pretending to be my mother. It was not uncommon for Jewish camp survivors, particularly those who had lost their own children, to come to the orphanage and offer to adopt us. Different Jewish organisations also encouraged adoptions in their publications. We older kids took special pride in refusing to be adopted, and since I for one was sure that my parents were alive and would soon find me, I had an even better reason to remain in the orphanage. The director tried to console me by suggesting that I might be mistaken about the letter. It could have been written in Polish for my mother by someone else, she suggested. After all, the letter was not addressed to me, she said, but to the orphanage, and my mother may have felt that a letter in German would not even be read. None of that convinced me, but as I ran out of her office in tears, I heard her say that she was not giving up yet and that I shouldn't either.

Weeks passed. I tried to put the letter out of my mind, but did not succeed. Because I was sure that the letter had not come from my mother I began to wonder why, if my parents were alive, they had not yet found me, more than a year after the end of the war. Once I asked myself that question I was forced to think the unthinkable: if so many other people had been murdered, wasn't it possible that my parents had also died? No! That I was not willing to admit. It simply could not be true! Gradually, though, I began to have doubts and wondered whether maybe only one of them had survived and, if so, whether it would have been my mother or my father. I knew that my mother had had some health problems in the ghetto – I learned later that she suffered from a thyroid condition – and I knew how good my father was at outsmarting the Germans. Those reflections convinced me that, if only one of them had survived, it would have been my father. But whichever it was should certainly have found me by now. In the past, before the letter, I had been able to avoid thinking about the fate of my parents by refusing to admit to myself that they might both be dead. Now it gradually dawned on me that I was probably all alone in the world and that there was not much I could do about it, other than go to Palestine. Suddenly, that prospect looked ever more tempting.

Knowing that it would be some time before I could leave the orphanage for Palestine, I tried to avoid thinking about my parents by spending more and more time playing soccer and table tennis. Then, one afternoon, while I was in the midst of an exciting soccer game, the director came running out of her office, waving a letter. I looked at it and immediately recognised my mother's unmistakable handwriting. It began, *Mein liebster Tommyli* – My dearest Tommyli. Right then and there I knew that she was alive. 'She is alive!' I kept repeating to myself. It was the happiest moment of my life. I began to cry and laugh all at once, casting off in a second the self-control and tough-guy attitude I had spent so much time cultivating at the orphanage. I had a mother, and that meant that I could be a child again.

If it had been today, rather than in 1946, that my mother had learned that I was alive, she would immediately have boarded a plane or train, travelled to Poland, and taken me back to Göttingen, her home town, to which she had returned after the war. But none of that was possible in 1946, nor was it possible for her to telephone me from Germany. It would have taken my mother many months to obtain the proper documents to travel to Poland. And since I had no passport, nor any other documents allowing me to leave Poland, more time would have been lost. It was thus readily apparent that other, less conventional, travel plans had to be put together to get me to her in Göttingen.

In the meantime, mail was the only way for us to communicate. But in those days it was slow and not always reliable. It took some four to six weeks for a letter from Germany to reach me in Otwock, if not longer, which meant that we were probably not able to exchange more than a few letters before we were reunited. Once I knew that she was alive, I was naturally becoming ever more impatient and frustrated, waiting to be with her. I can only imagine what she must have been going through at that same time. Oh, how I would have loved at least to have been able to hear her voice!

It was several months before we were reunited. Many people were involved in getting me from Otwock to Göttingen: the director of our orphanage, who was magnificent in pulling all the necessary bureaucratic strings, and various Jewish organisations, among them the American Joint Distribution Committee and Bricha. The latter was a secretive Jewish organisation that smuggled survivors from Europe to Palestine and, in the process, helped reunite families dispersed throughout Europe. To this day I don't know exactly who coordinated the various roles these organisations performed in getting me to my destination. What I do know is that my journey from Otwock, via Prague in Czechoslovakia and the American Zone in Germany, to Göttingen in the British Zone, with various stopovers along the way, was executed with admirable precision and without any hitches that I was aware of. It must have taken at least three or four weeks.

Such a journey, even in normal circumstances, would have required considerable coordination, since I was passed from one group or individual to another at different stages of the trip. Not only did I have to cross several borders, I had to cross them illegally because I lacked the proper papers. Some people were responsible for the border crossings, others for putting me up in temporary or clandestine Jewish transit centres and at times even in hotels. On the whole, the border crossings were not very perilous and were sometimes effected in plain view of guards who presumably had been bribed. Only one crossing involved more effort: trudging through deep snow in a forest at night while trying not to get caught. It might have been the Polish–Czech frontier or the border between Czecho-slovakia and the US Zone of Germany, I am not sure. What I do remember, though, is the cold. This particular border crossing took place either in late November or early December, and my feet, sensitive to the cold because of my earlier frostbite and amputations, hurt and made walking difficult. That in turn brought back unpleasant memories of the Auschwitz Death March. Fortunately it took only a few hours to make this cross-ing before we arrived at a warm transit centre.

With the exception of one border crossing, where I was the only person being brought over, I usually travelled in a group of between ten and twenty people – a 'transport', as our Bricha guides called it. The composition of these groups and their size changed from way station to way station. For example, we would arrive at a transit centre after we had crossed a border and find others already waiting there. That group would have priority over us in moving to the next destination, while we had to wait a few days more for our turn. Although it was all very efficiently organised, it took a lot of time to transport us from country to country.

One event from that voyage was vividly brought back to me in most dramatic fashion more than half a century later. After having been smuggled from Poland to Czechoslovakia, I was detached from my group and taken to Prague. There, I was placed in the care of a young American woman who put me up for about a week in an elegant hotel where she lived. She was very kind to me, took me to nice places to eat and showed me many interesting sights in the city. When the time came for me to leave Prague in order to join the transport that would take me to the American Zone of Germany, I promised that I would stay in touch. But I was not able to because, in the excitement of my anticipated reunion with my mother, I lost the piece of paper on which she had written her name and address. Then, on 19 March 2000, an email with the subject heading 'Is it you?' flashed on to my computer screen:

I read in the *Jerusalem Post* of March 6 about your
election to serve as World Court judge ... I am
wondering whether you are the same Tommy
Buergenthal who during the years 1946 or 1947 was

brought from Poland to Prague, by special escort, and
had to spend a few days in Prague, waiting ... to rejoin
his mother in Germany. If so, I was the welfare worker
of the American Joint Distribution Committee with
whom you stayed and who took care of you. My name
then was Freda Cohen ... Although more than 50 years
have elapsed, I have never forgotten the child or the
name Tommy Buergenthal, and often wondered about
your whereabouts. Seeing your name in print was a
most exciting experience for me, and I would be very
happy to hear whether you are in fact the same Tommy
Buergenthal.

The email was signed Freda (Cohen) Koren and it came from
Tel Aviv. Of course, I replied immediately. We corresponded for
a year and a half and made plans to get together in the near
future. Then, shortly after she advised me that she intended to
visit me in the Netherlands, I received the sad news of her sudden death; by then she was in her mid-eighties and had lived a
full life. At least I had been given the opportunity, after all those
many years, to thank her for taking such good care of me in
1946. I may have forgotten her name, but I had never forgotten
the kindness she had shown me. I had also thought of her
almost every time I walked through a revolving door. This
incongruous association between revolving doors and Freda, I
explained in my first email to her, was prompted by an experience I had when she brought me to her hotel. At the entrance

of the hotel, I came to an abrupt stop in front of such a door. I had never before seen one and it took me a while to figure out how one passed through such a contraption. 'That was obviously one piece of information I did not need to know in order to survive in the concentration camps,' I commented to her in that email, as we tried to catch up on developments in our lives that spanned a period of more than fifty-five years.

After I left Prague, I crossed the Czech frontier with another transport and entered the American Zone near the Bavarian city of Hof, where another transit centre awaited us. One more border remained, the one separating the British and American Zones, before I would be reunited with my mother in Göttingen. I passed through that border in a United States military train, accompanied by another representative of the American Joint. The date was 29 December 1946. Göttingen was just twenty kilometres away.

Once we had passed this last border, I got up from my seat and stood by the window until we rolled into Göttingen station. I could not contain my excitement. I spotted my mother even before the train came to a stop. As I try to describe the emotions of that moment, I realise that I am incapable of putting into words what I felt. And even now, so many years later, tears well up in my eyes as I see her standing there, nervously scanning the slowing train for a sight of me. While it was still moving I jumped out and raced over to her. We fell into each other's arms and stayed that way long after the train had moved out of the station, hugging each other and trying in just a few minutes to recount all that had happened to us since that August day in 1944 when we were separated in Auschwitz. 'Und Papa?' I finally asked. She did not answer right away, but kept shaking her head as tears ran down her cheeks. I knew then that my father had not survived the war that was now finally over for my mother and me.

Chapter 9

# A New Beginning

From the moment we were together again, Mutti and I talked and talked for days on end about everything that had happened to us during the two and a half years we had been separated. That is how I learned that in late 1944 she had been sent from Auschwitz to the notorious women's concentration camp of Ravensbrück, ninety kilometres from Berlin. Ravensbrück was evacuated by the SS ahead of the approaching Soviet troops towards the end of April 1945. Mutti and the other inmates able to walk were marched west until they reached Malchow, a satellite camp of Ravensbrück. Many of the women died on that march. On 28 April 1945 Malchow was liberated by the Soviets. Ironically, at that point, a mere sixty-odd kilometres separated Mutti and me, yet it took another year and a half for us to be reunited.

During the week following her liberation, Mutti and a small group of her friends stayed in various deserted German houses, helping themselves to the food and clothing they desperately needed. With the exception of Mutti, these women were all born in Poland and they decided to return to their home towns as soon as possible in the hope of finding surviving relatives. Mutti joined them, planning to get to Kielce, which was one of the meeting places she and my father had agreed upon if they survived the war. She also assumed, correctly as it turned out, that others who had survived the ghetto would be returning there and might provide information about my father and me in case we were not yet there.

Mutti reached Kielce after a horrendous journey by foot, truck and rail that took almost two weeks. With no money and no food other than what little she could scavenge or beg from farmers along the way, she arrived completely exhausted. During the trip, particularly after her little group had split up, she had to be very careful not to be taken for a German. Since she spoke very little Polish, she decided to claim that she was Hungarian if asked. She did not know a word of Hungarian, either, but reasoned that she was less likely to run into someone who would address her in that language. She was lucky on that score, and lucky too on the single occasion she gave away her German origin. That happened when someone stepped on her foot in the back of a very crowded truck and a mild German curse left her lips. Before she knew it she was pushed off the truck, but she was fortunate to have escaped a severe beating or worse.

Some of the survivors who returned to Kielce had established a Jewish community organisation. Mutti was welcomed with open arms, since most of the members knew her from the

labour camp and the Henryków factory. Provided with temporary shelter and food, she began to make inquiries about my
father and me. She soon learned from other survivors that after
my father and I had been separated in Auschwitz, he was sent
to Flossenbürg and had died there shortly before the end of the
war. For days, Mutti walked around in a stupor, unwilling to
believe what she had been told. But as more and more survivors returned to Kielce and confirmed the news of his death,
she had no choice but to accept it. (I found out only after the
first edition of this book was published that my father had in
fact been sent from Auschwitz to Sachsenhausen and from
there to Buchenwald, where he died on 15 January 1945. Ever
since I learned that our paths had crossed in Sachsenhausen, I
keep asking myself 'what if we had been reunited in Sachsenhausen?' Yes, what if ...?)

None of the returnees could tell her for sure what had happened to me. Many of them knew me well from Kielce and
Auschwitz, but no one had seen me after the liberation or near
that time. One person thought I might have been either on the
Auschwitz death transport or in Sachsenhausen, but was not
really sure. As Mutti kept prodding them to remember whether
they might not have seen me after the liberation of Sachsenhausen, they tried to convince her that I could not possibly be
alive. 'None of the children survived,' they reminded her gently. 'How could Tommy have? After all, he was by far the youngest from Kielce.' 'Now you must think of yourself and your
health,' they added, concerned by her fragile condition and her

nervous exhaustion. But she would have none of it. She knew that I was alive, for hadn't the fortune-teller proclaimed that I was a 'lucky child'?

When her search in Kielce yielded no further useful information, Mutti decided that the time had come to travel to Göttingen, which was another of the meeting places she and my father had agreed upon. Returning to Germany from Poland was no easier than her outward trip had been. Conditions along the roads were still as chaotic and dangerous as before, and transportation equally difficult to find. But with the help of some money she had received from the Jewish community in Kielce, Mutti eventually made it to Göttingen. On arrival she was utterly exhausted and lapsed into depression. She was hospitalised shortly after her arrival and treated for her now-acute thyroid condition. The doctors also prescribed complete rest. This was before tranquillisers, so Mutti was simply given plenty of sleeping pills.

By the time Mutti left the hospital, several weeks later, she had regained some of her strength. It was not easy for her to find herself back in the Göttingen she remembered from her once happy childhood and then from the Nazi period. Almost as soon as the Nazis had come to power most of Mutti's non-Jewish school friends acted as if they had never known her. They would cross the street when they saw her approaching or look the other way to avoid greeting her. She was treated even more shabbily on the only two occasions she returned to Göttingen from Lubochna to visit my grandparents and show me off, her new baby. Now, after the war, these same women embraced her on the street and acted as if the past had never happened.

On the Gronerstrasse, one of the town's two main streets where my grandparents' home and shoe store had been located, the original sign – 'Schuhgeschäft Paul Silbergleit' – could still be seen faintly under the painted-over name of the new owner, to whom my grandparents had been forced to sell their home for a pittance. Mutti was born and grew up in that house, and now all that remained of that past and of her family's life in Göttingen were those rapidly fading letters spelling out her father's name. It is not surprising that, in those early days in Göttingen, she frequently wondered whether having survived the camps was just another punishment she did not deserve.

During that very difficult period, and as she agonised over the fact that there was no news of me, Mutti was approached one day by an old lady who asked her to help her cross one of the busy Göttingen streets. Turning on the poor thing, Mutti screamed, 'Nobody ever helped my mother across the street in this damn town!' and walked off. Years later, once the past had gradually lost its painful immediacy, Mutti would frequently recall 'her shameful behaviour', as she characterised it. It kept bothering her that she had been so terribly mean to that woman. 'After all,' she would ask, 'how could I blame the old lady for what the Nazis had done to my mother?'

Not long after leaving the hospital Mutti walked into the bakery next to where her parents' store had been. She was immediately recognised and lovingly embraced by Mrs Appel,

The Silbergeits' home in Göttingen with the shoe shop
on the ground floor

the baker's wife. Despite Nazi orders not to fraternise with Jews, the Appels had continued to maintain contact with my grandparents and helped them whenever they could. After a happy and tearful reunion with Mutti, Mrs Appel told her that she had something for her. She disappeared and returned a few minutes later carrying a dust-covered suitcase. 'Your parents left this with us for safe keeping,' Mrs Appel told Mutti as she handed it to her. 'We were always afraid that the Nazis would find it and punish us, but we promised your parents to hide it and we did.' The suitcase contained some tablecloths and sheets, as well as a few pieces of silver. Near the bottom of the suitcase Mutti found a batch of family photographs and some letters my grandparents had received from her and her brother Eric in America. For Mutti, the pictures were a treasure trove. All her family photos, including those of her parents, my father and me, had been lost in the camps. Erased with their destruction, it seemed to her, was proof that her family had ever existed. Now Mutti could again look at those images of a happier life long ago, before the Nazis destroyed it. It was the first good thing that had happened to her since her return.

Housing was very difficult to come by in Göttingen after the war. The city had not been bombed, but its population had almost doubled following the influx of a large number of German refugees who had lost their homes in the east. Mutti had been assigned a very small and dark apartment, which she found cramped and depressing. Her problem was solved one day when she ran into Mr Fritz Schügl, whom she knew as the owner of a jewellery store located one street down from my grandparents' shop. He wanted to know whether she needed a place to stay and offered her an apartment on the second floor of his family home. Housing and rentals generally were very strictly controlled in those days, but concentration camp survivors were given preference and were entitled to better accommodation. As Mutti moved into the sunny apartment with a large balcony overlooking the Schügl garden her spirits improved dramatically, and with them her health.

Throughout this period Mutti never gave up hope that she would find me. She contacted the many search bureaus in Germany and elsewhere that had sprung up after the war to help reunite families. She was also in touch with those Kielce survivors whose addresses she had been able to obtain, hoping to hear from anyone who had seen me or might have information of my whereabouts. In one of the letters she found in the suitcase Mrs Appel had hidden for my grandparents, Mutti came across her brother Eric's address in the United States and immediately got in touch with him. Until then, he did not know that his sister had survived, nor what had happened to their parents. He also learned that my father had not survived and that Mutti was still looking for me. Eric immediately contacted various Jewish organisations in the United States and in Palestine, seeking their help in finding me.

Despite all the negative responses she received and suggestions from friends that I could not possibly have survived and that she should face this sad reality for her own peace of mind,

Mutti insisted that I was alive. 'I know that he is alive, I can feel it,' she would say. 'It is only a matter of time before I find him'. She was dramatically confirmed in that conviction by a blurred photograph she happened to see in a newspaper. According to the photo's caption, it showed a British soldier in Berlin walking with a group of liberated Jewish children. In that picture, Mutti was sure that she recognised me. 'Here is the proof I've been waiting for,' she told her friends as she displayed the cutting to all who had doubted that I could have survived. Although I was in Berlin at roughly that time, I never saw a British soldier there, nor was I one of the children pictured. But Mutti did not know that at the time, which was good, for the picture sustained her in her belief that I was alive and gave her the hope she needed in those difficult days.

More than half a year after returning to Göttingen Mutti learned that Dr Leon Reitter, with whom she had worked in Henryków, had survived the war and was in a displaced persons camp in the American Zone near Dachau, the concentration camp from which he had been liberated by American troops. Born in Poland, he was a paediatrician who had received his medical training in Czechoslovakia because only a very limited number of Jews were in those days allowed to study medicine in Poland. My parents and I came to know him in the ghetto; he was the doctor they called whenever I had a fever or some other ailment that needed attention. Dr Reitter's only daughter had been killed along with the other children after the Kielce labour camp was liquidated. Dr Reitter and my father became close friends and spent many hours in the evenings in Henryków talking about the course of the war and what the future had in store for us. Mutti was, of course, overjoyed that Dr Reitter was alive and invited him to Göttingen. Although it was not easy in those days to move from one zone of Germany to the other, he eventually made it. Not long afterwards they decided to get married. When I arrived in Göttingen, Dr Reitter was by her side at the station.

No sooner had we arrived from the Göttingen railroad station to the apartment in the Schügl house than I began to ask hundreds of questions and so did Mutti. The questions just rolled out and some of the answers produced tears in us both, but we were impatient to know what each of us had gone through in the more than two years of our separation. I heard more details about my father's death, about Mutti's death march out of Ravensbrück, about Dr Reitter's liberation from Dachau and about the transport from Auschwitz to Germany that he and my father were on after we were separated. One group from that transport was shipped to Dachau and the other to Flossenbürg.

Of course, I also wanted to know how Mutti had found me in Otwock. It appears that, true to her word, Lola, my counsellor in the orphanage, had placed my name on the list of kids from the orphanage who wanted to emigrate to Palestine. The list was transmitted to the Jewish Agency for Palestine. In the meantime, my uncle Eric in the United States had sent my name to a search bureau which the Agency maintained. Despite the fact that millions of people were searching for lost relatives and friends, an employee of the Jewish Agency found, among the vast numbers of research requests received by his office, a letter stating that a Mrs Gerda Buergenthal in Germany was looking for her child, Thomas. He then somehow remembered that, days earlier, he had seen that very name on a list of children in an orphanage in Poland who wanted to be brought to Palestine. Considering that the person at the Jewish Agency was performing this search manually in those pre-computer days, it borders on the miraculous that he managed in this fashion to make the connection between my mother and me. It is not surprising, therefore, that whenever Mutti told the story of how we were reunited, she declared that it had been *beschert* (preordained). 'After all,' she would proclaim, 'the fortune-teller in Katowice already predicted it.'

The Jewish Agency immediately informed my uncle Eric, who contacted my mother. Unable to travel to Poland after hearing that I was alive, and afraid to write to me in German, Mutti asked Dr Reitter to write to the orphanage in Polish. That was the letter I was convinced had been sent by someone who wanted to adopt me. In the meantime, at the request of my uncle, the American Joint Distribution Committee embarked on its efforts to reunite me with my mother.

Some ten years later, on her first visit to Israel, Mutti passed a building identified as the headquarters of the Jewish Agency. Without a moment's hesitation she went in and asked to speak to someone in charge. She then explained that she had come to thank the Agency for reuniting her with her son. While no one remembered the case of the boy in the Otwock orphanage who found his mother with the Agency's help, she was given a joyous reception because, she was told, this was the first time anyone had come to thank the Agency for bringing a family together.

# Chapter 10

# Life in Germany

When I arrived in Germany at the end of December 1946 I was twelve and a half years old. During my first few days there I did not let Mutti out of my sight. I kept kissing her and holding on to her, anxious to assure myself that I was not just dreaming and that we were really together again. It was such a wonderful feeling to be with my mother, to know that I was no longer alone in this world, that she loved me and would take care of me. Almost as soon as I first embraced her at the station I felt that a tremendous burden had been lifted from my shoulders and put on hers: now Mutti was once again responsible for me. As I reflect on this attitude, I realise that it was probably a product of the selfish sentiments of a child: until then, I had been responsible for my own life, for my survival; I could not afford to depend on anyone but myself; I had to think and act like a grown-up and be constantly on the alert against all possible dangers. But once I was back in her arms I could be a child again, leaving these worries and concerns to her.

During the time I was separated from Mutti my German had become rather rusty, but within a week or two of coming to

*Thomas shortly after his arrival in Göttingen*

Göttingen I was once again comfortable speaking the language and even lost the slight Polish accent Mutti claimed I had acquired while in the Polish army and at Otwock. It helped that young Fritz Schügl, the son of our landlord, was only a couple of years older than I, and we became inseparable friends in no time.

From our balcony on the Wagnerstrasse I could look over the garden on to the street below. The street – Hainholzweg – was a popular pedestrian route leading to the countryside above the city. It attracted many residents of Göttingen, particularly on Sundays, when entire German families would pass our house during their outings. I would observe them from our balcony with envy and hatred. Here were fathers and mothers, grandfathers and grandmothers, walking with their children and grandchildren – people who, for all I knew, had killed my father and grandparents! As I contemplated these scenes of happy Germans enjoying their lives as if nothing had happened in the recent past, I longed to have a machine gun mounted on the balcony with which I could do to them what they had done to my family. It took me a long time to get over these sentiments and recognise that such indiscriminate acts of vengeance would not bring my father or grandparents back to life. It took me even longer to recognise that the only way to protect mankind against crimes such as those that were visited upon us is to break the cycle of hatred and violence that invariably leads to ever more suffering by innocent human beings.

By the time I arrived in Göttingen I had received at most half a year of formal education, all of it in the Polish school in Otwock, so was ill prepared to attend a German school with kids of my own age. Mutti found a retired teacher who agreed to tutor me privately for a little over a year. During that year, I made up the six or seven years of school I had missed. My tutor, Otto Biedermann, had been expelled from Upper Silesia when it was taken over by Poland and had come to Göttingen as a refugee. He was a wonderful teacher who, more than any I had thereafter, introduced me to the joy of learning. I went to him every morning for two hours and in the afternoons I did the homework he gave me.

Initially, of course, he had to teach me how to read and write – the basics of what children learn in the first couple of grades – before he could introduce me to all the other material I would have learned had I been able to attend school like other children my age, who at that point had already completed some six years of their formal education. That meant that Mr Biedermann had to make sure that I covered the following subjects, among others: German, English, history, geography and mathematics.

To improve my reading skills, Mr Biedermann introduced me to the books of Karl May, the famous writer of 'Wild West' stories that have captivated German children since the late nineteenth century. My reading skills improved dramatically as I devoured these books, learning all about cowboys and Indians and the American frontier from an author who had never set foot on that continent, but whose imagination and research made up for his lack of first-hand knowledge. His books were filled with suspense, making it very difficult for me to put them down. Once I had significantly improved my reading skills with Karl May's books, it proved easier for Mr Biedermann to get me to read other books and thus, gradually, to introduce me to the works of German literature that I would have been studying at school. To improve my writing I had to produce a brief essay every morning, describing what I had seen on the way from my home to his. Under normal circumstances, it would take me about fifteen minutes or so to walk to his house. I soon ran out of anything new to report, so began to vary my route, rising earlier every morning and finding new ways to get there. This took me to parts of town I had never seen before. I encountered all kinds of people in the streets and would try to guess who they were and where they were going. In those days, the streets of Göttingen, like those of other German cities, still provided ample evidence of the terrible human suffering the war had visited on ordinary Germans. I would see amputees, people whose faces had been horribly disfigured by burns in the most bizarre ways and some who had been blinded in one eye or both. Many of these individuals still wore all or part of their faded military uniforms. I would pass people who, judging from their demeanour and clothing, looked like refugees. These daily discoveries made it easier to write the essays Mr Biedermann demanded of me and led to some interesting discussions about contemporary realities that would never have been touched upon in school.

Mr Biedermann once told Mutti that teaching me was an experience like none he had ever had. On the one hand, he told her, I was a child who lacked even the most rudimentary educational background and needed to be tutored as if I were a six-year-old; on the other, I had the life experience and maturity of an adult and could discuss subjects that no child my age would usually know of or be interested in. While learning German and European history I would ask him about life during the Nazi period and why he thought the Nazis had come to power, if he had known any Nazis and what kind of people they were. I wanted to know about his expulsion from Upper Silesia and whether he blamed the Poles or Hitler for what had happened to him and the other refugees. When studying geography we talked about places I knew, countries I might want to live in, what the people there were like, the food they grew and the animals they kept. Learning was fun with Mr Biedermann and I missed that sort of lesson very much when I eventually entered school a year later. The only subject Mr Biedermann did not feel competent to teach me was mathematics – but since I had no interest in or talent for maths, I was pleased that we neglected that subject for some time until Mutti eventually found a university student to coach me. That apart, Mr Biedermann provided me with six years' education in just over twelve months.

When I returned to Göttingen for a brief visit some years after emigrating to the United States, one of the first people I wanted to see was my old tutor. I had so much to tell him. He was interested in a great many things and I knew that he would want to hear about my studies in America, about my life there, about the books I was reading and so on. When I called his home, however, I learned that he had had a stroke and was in hospital. So, I went to visit him there. He recognised me as I walked into his room and, though he could not speak, he squeezed my hand and held on to it for a long time. I am sure that he knew that I had come not only to say goodbye, but to thank him for laying the intellectual foundation of the life I was destined to live.

There were two secondary boys' schools in Göttingen in my time (in those days schools were still segregated by gender): one specialised in classical studies such as Latin and ancient Greek; the other, which is now known as the Felix-Klein-Gymnasium, focused on modern languages and contemporary subjects. When Mr Biedermann decided that I was ready for school,

I opted for the Felix-Klein-Gymnasium and was enrolled there in 1948. Thanks to Mr Biedermann's lessons I was admitted to the grade that I would have been in had I received a normal education. That made it much easier for me to become fully integrated into the life of the school.

I was the only Jewish student in the school. That had one great advantage: it meant that I was allowed to play in the school yard during the one or two hours a week that religion was taught. As a rule, a Protestant clergyman or theologian would teach this course to the Protestant students in my class, and a Catholic priest to the Catholic students. I was excused from the religion course because, it was explained to me, there was no rabbi in town who could teach me. Of course, I was delighted not to have to attend any religion classes. Not surprisingly, some of my classmates envied my special status, since they, too, would have loved to have been excused from taking religion.

None of my classmates had ever met a Jew but, as some told me later, they had seen Nazi cartoons depicting Jews as dark-skinned alien-looking people with long crooked noses, black beards and rapacious faces that were intended, because of their caricatured ugliness, to illustrate the repulsive character of Jews. That is probably why some of my classmates asked, on first learning that I was Jewish, whether I really was a Jew for, as they put it, 'You do not look like one.' Others were surprised that I was good at sports, quite strong and not afraid to defend myself when challenged by the class bullies. They had obviously been exposed to Nazi propaganda which described Jews as weaklings, cowards and lacking all aptitude in sports. Soon, though, after the initial awkwardness of our encounter and the novelty of having 'a real Jew' in their class, I was accepted by my classmates as one of them and, what is more, I gradually came to feel that I was indeed one of them. I never heard any anti-Semitic remarks from my fellow students, not even when I got into the typical schoolboy shoving matches with one or the other of them, nor did I ever sense that they harboured anti-Semitic feelings that they were hiding from me. But as I reflect now on those years, I am struck by the fact that I do not remember any of my classmates or my teachers asking about my life in German concentration camps, despite the fact that it was no secret that I spent the war years in these camps. Was it that they did not want to hear about my past or did they believe that I would find it painful to talk about it? I simply do not know.

Although my classmates accepted me, I could not help but feel that my presence made some of my teachers rather uncomfortable. Many of them had been members of the Nazi Party. After the war they had to submit to the denazification process instituted by the occupation authorities and required clearance before being allowed to teach again. I do not know how many former teachers had failed to pass this process, but the impression at the time was that many a real Nazi – in contrast to the innocuous 'Mitläufer' or fellow-travellers, those who had joined the Nazi Party not out of conviction but for economic or other reasons – slipped through the denazification net and were frequently reinstated. In these early post-war years most of these people were afraid to voice their opinions. It was not surprising, therefore, that I was not subjected to any overt anti-Semitism, although I sensed that some of them were always on guard because I was in their class and because of their own past. They carefully avoided expressing their own opinions on certain 'sensitive' issues that came up in the classroom. I had the feeling, and that is all it was, that some of them may have been denazified without ever eschewing their Nazi views. Only once did some of these sentiments come to the fore. During a class discussion, and I no longer remember in which class it was, the teacher burst out with an harangue about the Allied bombing of Hamburg and the large loss of life. It was barbaric and unprecedented, he claimed. I raised my hand and asked, 'What about the German bombing of London? Shouldn't we also speak about that? And what about all the people who were murdered in Nazi concentration camps?' The man turned crimson and gave some explanation that equated the concentration camps to the Allied bombings, which prompted me to walk out of the classroom, a totally unheard of act of rebellion in a German school in those days. My mother, of course, immediately complained to the school's director and the teacher eventually apologised, saying that I had misunderstood him. It was clear to me, though, that he apologised only for fear of losing his job. One of my mother's friends who had lived in Göttingen during the war chided her for not seeking the teacher's dismissal because the man was, as her friend put it, '*ein alter Nazi*' (an old Nazi) who should never have been allowed to teach again.

We learned a great deal of history in our school, but it was mainly ancient and medieval German and European history. Contemporary history was simply ignored. Not only was the Second World War, its causes and the rise of Hitler not discussed, but even the First World War, if I remember correctly, seemed too modern a subject to be dealt with. That was in sharp contrast, of course, to the impressive efforts made in later years by the West German education authorities, who drastically revised their school curricula to permit and encourage students to confront the past honestly and to foster a democratic spirit of openness. Regrettably, that was not the case when I was at school in Göttingen. I was struck by the difference when I came to the United States and enrolled in an American high school. Being used to the oppressive discipline that in those days still reigned in German schools, I found the atmosphere in my American school almost too free and undisciplined. What most impressed me, though, was the freedom that American teachers tolerated and encouraged when it came to the expression of student views on almost any subject under discussion. We also had a large number of student clubs and associations with elected officers in my American high school; a school-wide student government with a panoply of officers; and annual elections for all those offices with election campaigns, pamphlets and speeches mirroring American political elections. Whatever one might think of the academic quality of

American high-school education, the American classroom struck me as a veritable incubator of a democratic way of life, something the German classroom in my day certainly was not.

I spent a great deal of my free time in Göttingen playing sports. I joined a table tennis club and a sports club, and played soccer to exhaustion with Fritz Schügl and other boys from school and the neighbourhood. I swam in the city's outdoor pool and in an abandoned stone quarry that was supposed to be off-limits. Fritz and I explored the countryside on our bikes and spent hours cleaning and oiling them. After I developed an interest in girls, we would join our classmates in the evenings, parading up and down the main street while ogling the girls and trying to arrange dates with them. There were parties and dancing and some drinking. In short, I lived the very normal life of a German teenager.

There were only a handful of Jews in Göttingen when I arrived there. Most of them were quite elderly. The unelected leader of this minuscule Jewish community was Richard Gräfenberg, the scion of one of the oldest, perhaps the oldest, Göttingen Jewish families whose ancestors had received a *Freibrief* (licence), allowing them to settle in the town as early as the late Middle Ages. Mr Gräfenberg, who by the time I met him was very old, had been able to live peacefully in Göttingen throughout the war, apparently because his wife was not Jewish and also because she had good connections to the town's Gestapo chief. Gräfenberg had been able to keep his family home, a large house with a beautiful garden and many fruit trees. From time to time I was allowed to pick some of the apples, pears and plums that grew there, a special privilege in those days when almost everything edible was in scarce supply.

Mutti, who acted as Mr Gräfenberg's deputy community leader – that sounds almost funny now, considering that there were probably no more than six or seven Jews in town, including us – had to visit him every month in connection with the distribution of the food packages the community received from the American Joint Distribution Committee. They had to be picked up from Hildesheim, the town's district seat, or from the former concentration camp of Bergen-Belsen, which functioned as a displaced persons' camp at the time. It was Mutti's job to make these trips, and I would occasionally accompany her. The packages contained not only foodstuffs but also American cigarettes and coffee, both highly valued black-market commodities in those early post-war days. These could be traded for just about anything, from butter and meat to Persian rugs and jewellery. The people distributing the packages in Hildesheim or Bergen-Belsen not only tried to cheat us but would at the same time suggest that Mutti was a fool not to claim that there were more Jews living in Göttingen and keep the surplus for herself. That would make her terribly angry, and on the way back she would always complain that the wrong people had survived the camps. It annoyed her even more when I reminded her that we, too, had survived. Of course, she was thinking of my father. If he had lived, she said, he would long ago have cleared those thieves out of the distribution centres. After Mr Gräfenberg died, Mutti succeeded him as president.

As soon as I had arrived in Göttingen, Dr Reitter became my surrogate father. He was a gentle, kind and most patient human being whom I came to love and admire. He helped me with my homework, taught me how to study and encouraged me to read and to discuss what I had read. I was also very much attracted to his extensive medical library, particularly the anatomy and dermatology books with pictures of naked women which I studied surreptitiously when no one was around. Although Dr Reitter had been a paediatrician in Poland, he decided to specialise in dermatology in Göttingen because, as he put it, 'Paediatrics is too strenuous a medical speciality for someone with my heart problems who no longer has the strength to make house calls.' I had noticed that he would swallow some heart medication from time to time, particularly when we had to walk uphill from town towards the Wagnerstrasse where we lived.

Once in a while he would take me to visit the University's dermatology clinic, show me the wards where patients with venereal diseases were housed, explain how they were contracted and the gruesome effects they could have. I loved those excursions and decided that I would one day study medicine. In the meantime I used to practise writing my signature in the German way with the title – Dr med. Thomas Buergenthal – I expected to earn.

*Dr Leon Reitter, 1947*

Our excursions to these clinics became less and less frequent. I noticed that whenever we had to walk up even the smallest incline, Dr Reitter would have to stop often and take his heart pills. He complained of chest pain and found it increasingly hard to breathe after the slightest exertion. As that pain got worse, his cardiologist decided to have him admitted to hospital; I believe he may have suffered a minor heart attack, too. Mutti, who had never had any experience of heart disease, thought at first that he was exaggerating the problem, but once she realised how serious his condition was she not only worried day and night about his health but threw all her energy into aiding his recovery. In those pre-bypass, pre-angioplasty days, the doctors could prescribe only rest and more rest to help his condition. He was also given a variety of injections, but nothing seemed to work. Whenever I went to visit him, we would talk about his recovery prospects, which he felt were increasingly bleak. From time to time he would draw a picture of his heart and show me where his blood vessels were blocked and why his heart did not work as it should. Sometimes, when a nurse was very busy, he would show me how to give him an injection – it was usually morphine – and I became quite good at dispensing it.

He was getting weaker by the day. Fluid began to accumulate in his lungs. During one visit he told me that he would soon die and that it would then be up to me to take good care of Mutti, though I was not to tell her that the end was near. Not long after that Dr Reitter died peacefully in his sleep. This was the second time I had lost a father and Mutti a husband. At that point we both decided that there was no God in heaven, for what kind of God would permit such a good man to die so young – he was only forty-eight years old – and cause so much suffering to be visited on one small family.

It took Mutti and me a long time to get over Dr Reitter's death, if we ever did. Her thyroid condition began to trouble her again and she developed an irregular heartbeat. We tried to console each other without much success, but we both knew that life had to go on and that we had to make the best of it. Our daily routine was interrupted one afternoon by an event that brought some happiness and excitement into our lives. Not long after I had arrived in Göttingen from Otwock, I told Mutti and Dr Reitter about the Norwegian who had helped me so much in the Sachsenhausen infirmary and who probably saved my life.

Although I had forgotten his name by then, I remembered that one day he had pointed to the picture of a man on the side of the jar of cookies he'd brought and said that it was his father. Perhaps my friend was the son of a cookie manufacturer, suggested Mutti, adding that it was most unlikely that I would ever find him. But then, sometime in early 1948, Mutti saw an article in a newsletter published by an organisation of former concentration camp inmates. The article reported that a Norwegian by the name of Odd Nansen, son of the famous Norwegian explorer and statesman Fridtjof Nansen, had recently published the diary he had kept in various camps, including Sachsenhausen. It had become the most widely read book in Norway.* After showing me the article, Mutti suggested that I write to the author of the book and ask whether he could help me find the person who had been so kind to me in Sachsenhausen.

I did just that. My letter to him began as follows:

Dear Mr Nansen: Please forgive me for disturbing you. A few days ago we read an article which pointed out that the most widely read book in Norway was your diary about your three-year incarceration in Sachsenhausen. I was also in Sachsenhausen. My name is Tommy

---

*Odd Nansen's three-volume diaries, Fra Dag til Dag, were first published in Norway in 1947. Two English-language abridged versions of this book were published in the United States (From Day to Day) and Great Britain (Day after Day) in 1949. A much shorter German translation of the book, Von Tag zu Tag, was also published in 1949.

Buergenthal and I was 10 years old at the time. I was in
the *Revier*, where two of my toes were amputated.

Then I told him about the Norwegian I had met there, that he
had been very kind to me and helped me very much, but that I
had forgotten his name and lost his address. In the last para-
graph of my letter I said that I had found my mother after a
two-year separation, and continued:

> The name Nansen sounds most familiar to me and that
> is why I am writing this letter to you. Could you possibly
> be that certain person? In case you are not, I would like
> to ask you to inquire among your circle of friends who
> that person could have been so that I might thank him.

Since I did not have the address of the author of the diaries,
I simply put 'Mr Odd Nansen, Norway' on the envelope and
mailed it off.

Weeks passed without an answer. In time I forgot all about
the letter. Then one day our doorbell rang. When I opened the
door, I was greeted by a Norwegian soldier who had arrived in
a military truck. (At that time there was a small Norwegian garrison stationed in the British Zone of Germany.) Pointing to
the truck, he said that he had a 'package' to deliver. When I
suggested that he give it to me, he said it was too big for me to
carry. At that point, two other soldiers jumped off the truck and
opened its rear flap. They pulled out a huge wooden crate and

carried it into the house, up the stairs and into our apartment. 'This is from Odd Nansen,' one of the soldiers said as he handed me a letter. The letter began with 'Lieber, lieber Tommy!' And it continued:

You cannot imagine the great happiness your letter produced in me and many, many others ... That is how we learned for the first time that you were alive and had found your mother. Your letter made your many old friends very happy, as well as the many new friends you now have without knowing it ... First, I have to tell you that I am 'that certain person' who visited you in the *Revier* in Sachsenhausen. Moreover, in my diaries, which you already know about, I devote a number of chapters to you and to our conversations in the *Revier*, where I met you and where I and many of my comrades came to love you and could never forget you. Many thousands of people have now read my diaries and many of them think they know you because of that book. They have frequently asked me whether I had heard anything about little Tommy, but again and again I had to disappoint them.

Mr Nansen then told me of his long and unsuccessful search for me and his gradual acceptance that I had not survived. But my letter changed all that. To know that I was alive and that I had been reunited with my mother was marvellous news for

**ODD NANSEN**

ARKITEKT

Angekommen den 7.II.48.

WERGELANDSVEIEN 7
TELEFON 33 02 64

OSLO , den 4.2.1948

Lieber, lieber Tommy !

Du weisst garnicht, welch' grosse Freude Du mir und vielen, vielen anderen durch Deinen Brief bereitest hast, wofür
ich Dir herzlichst danke. Erstens bekamen wir dadurch zu hören,
dass Du lebst und Deine Mutter wiedergefunden hast. Und für
alle Deine Freunde, Du hast noch und nach noch viele dazube-
kommen, wovon Du keine Ahnung hast, war es eine unsäglich grosse
Freude. Siehst Du, Tommy, das hängt folgendermassen zusammen:
Zuerst einmal war ich "der betreffende Herr", der Dich im Revier
von Sachsenhausen besuchte, und in meinem Tagebuch, wovon Du ja
selbst gehört hast, habe ich mehrere Kapitel um Dich geschrie-
ben, um meine Gespräche mit Dir während der Besuche im Revier, wo
ich Dich kennengelernt und Dich, sowie viele andere Gefangenen-
kameraden so lieb gewonnen haben, dass wir Dich nie mehr verges-
sen können. Dieses Tagebuch wurde von Tausenden von Menschen
gelesen und vielen scheint es, Dich dadurch zu kennen. Sie haben
Dich natürlich genau so lieb gewonnen wie wir. Ständig haben sie
mich gefragt, ob ich nichts mehr über den kleinen Tommy gehört
habe, aber immer wieder musste ich sie durch mein Kopfschütteln
enttäuschen. Während der Zeit, die seit dem Kriegsende vergangen
ist, habe ich überall versucht herauszubekommen, ob Du nach dem
Kriege aus Sachsenhausen mit dem Leben davongekommen bist und wo
Du Dich zufällig aufhältst. Alle Nachforschungen waren leider ver-
gebens. Wir mussten nach und nach glauben, Du lebst nicht mehr.
Ich bin gerade auf einer langen Reisedurch Europa gewesen und
habe überall wo ich glaubte, es gäbe eine Möglichkeit, eine Spur
von Dir zu finden, Untersuchung eingeleitet, aber leider ohne
Ergebnis. Du kannst Dir deswegen vorstellen, wie gross die Freude
für mich war, Deinen Brief auf meinem Schreibtisch nach meiner
Rückkehr zu finden. Jetzt kann ich all denen, die nach Dir fragen,
mit Freude antworten und ihnen die leuchtende frohe Botschaft
überbringen: Tommy lebt! Tommy wohnt in Göttingen zusammen mit
seiner Mutter.

Auch meine Frau und meine Kinder, ich habe vier Kinder,
sowohl älter und auch jünger als Du. Sie jubelten vor Freude,
als ich ihnen Deinen Brief laut vorlese, denn sie denkten auch
oft an Dich und wünschten sich so innig dass es gelingen möge,
Dich wiederzufinden. Und so lebst Du ja, sozusagen mitten unter
uns und hast noch dazu Deine Mutter wiedergefunden. Das klingt ja
wie ein unglaubliches, leuchtendes und gutes Märchen mitten in der
Elendigkeit in der Welt. Hätte ich nur gewusst, dass Du lebst und
in Göttingen wohnst, Du kannst sicher sein, ich hätte Dich auf
meiner neulichen Tur durch Deutschland aufgesucht. Ich kam auch
durch Hannover, welches ja nicht so schrecklich lang von Göttingen
liegt.

Letter from Odd Nansen to Thomas Buergenthal

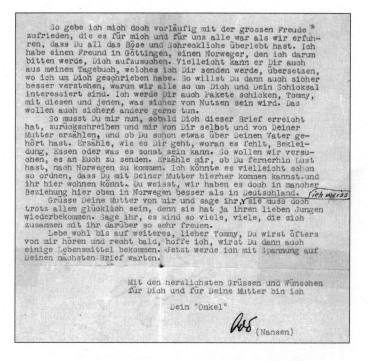

him, his family and my many old and new friends. He asked
me to write straight away and to tell him all about myself and
my mother and whether I had found my father. He also wanted
to know if we needed anything, particularly food and clothing,
and he offered to help us move to Norway, where living conditions at the time were better than in Germany. The letter was
signed, 'Your "Uncle" Odd (Nansen)'.

As we started to open the wooden crate I kept chiding
Mutti. 'I told you his father was not a cookie manufacturer!
Nobody believed that I would find him or that my letter would

reach him. See, it reached him even without a proper address,'
I gloated. The crate was filled with the most wondrous food:
cans of sardines and herring, condensed milk, dried fruit,
rice, flour and sugar, a variety of crackers, and many, many
chocolate bars and other such goodies. Mutti and I just stood
in total disbelief. Who had ever seen so much food, or even
tasted it? At the time, food was still severely rationed in Germany and even with the packages we received from the American Joint we never had enough, nor anything as exotic as this
shipment. We were in seventh heaven and, in the days to
come, ate more chocolate than was good for us. Later I learned
that Norwegian schoolchildren had collected the chocolate
and candy for me. They started their campaign after Norwegian newspapers reported that I was alive and living in Göttingen. Because Odd Nansen had dedicated his book to 'the
living memory' of some of his friends from camp and to 'you
too, little Tommy!' and had described me in his book as the
'Angel Raphael of the Revier', I had become famous in Norway and something of a hero to the country's children. In the
meantime, the three-volume memoir arrived with the following inscription:

Dear Tommy, here is my camp diary. As you will see, it
is also dedicated to you. Even though you will not be
able to read it in Norwegian, I want you nevertheless to
have it as a present from a person who came to love you
and one who never forgot nor ever will forget his young

friend, that little brave angel from Revier No. III in Sachsenhausen.

Some time later Odd Nansen came to Göttingen and arranged for me to visit him and his family in Norway. It was not all that easy for me to make that trip because I did not have a proper passport. After Mutti returned to Göttingen she was offered her German citizenship back, but she declined, telling the official who had come to see her, 'You took it away, now you can keep it!' So we did not have a German or any other passport. I eventually obtained a stateless passport and a visa for travel to Norway. Mutti and I met Mr Nansen in Hamburg, from where he and I flew to Oslo. At the airport Mr Nansen introduced me to a German he identified as 'my good friend, Mr Willy Brandt, who fought against the Nazis in the Norwegian resistance'. Of course, at the time, I had no idea that Willy Brandt was to become one of Germany's most famous chancellors, though years later I would proudly claim long acquaintance with him!

My trip to Norway was filled with one excitement after another. For one thing, I had never flown in an aeroplane before, which in itself was a thrilling experience. I arrived to a press conference at Oslo airport, where I had to answer hundreds of questions. Mr and Mrs Nansen and their four children – Marit, Eigil, Siri and Odd Erik – treated me like a beloved, long-lost family member. I also met up with many former inmates of Sachsenhausen whom I had known from the camp, among them – if I

*Drawing of the 'Raphael Angel of the Revier' in Tommy,*
*by Odd Nansen*

remember correctly – a prime minister and various other high government officials and celebrities. I felt very important, of course, although I most enjoyed being able to swim with the Nansen children in the Oslo fjord which abutted the family property. I had never even been near the sea, and the fjord with its surrounding mountains made it a very special experience for me. I also went with the Nansen family to their cottage in the mountains. Mr Nansen was an architect by profession and an excellent artist. His camp diary contained many sketches of inmates and Nazi guards, and his home in Oslo was filled with these and other paintings and drawings. Fun conversations and

*Thomas with Odd Nansen in 1951*

reminiscences enlivened our dinners. I even learned some Norwegian words because it was decreed that one day a week all conversation at dinner would be in Norwegian and, if I wanted to eat, I had to ask for the food in that language. That proved to be a strong incentive to learn the necessary words.

The only bad part of the trip was the return leg. Some American friends of the Nansens were scheduled to travel by train to Copenhagen via Sweden on the same day I was to leave Oslo. The Nansens thought that it would be fun for me to see the city, and especially the Tivoli, in the company of their friends as I made my way back to Germany. My plane ticket was traded in for a train ticket and we were on our way. But I did not get very far. I was stopped at the border between Norway and Sweden. Since I did not have transit visas for Sweden and Denmark, which I needed as a stateless person, I was not allowed to proceed. That meant that I had to return to Oslo, where the Nansens obtained the necessary visas for me. Back in Göttingen, about six weeks later and without ever having stopped to see Copenhagen, I told Mutti what problems I had encountered with my stateless passport. She was quite upset that her stand on a matter of principle should have caused me added hardship. 'To hell with principle,' she said, and a day later applied for the return of our German citizenship.

When the German translation of Odd Nansen's book appeared in 1949, he noted in the introduction that he was donating the proceeds of that edition to a fund set up to help German refugees. That made me wonder why a man who had spent more than three years in a Nazi concentration camp would care about the fate of these people. After some time I began to think that it was important that individuals such as Nansen and the rest of us who had been subjected to terrible suffering at the hands of the Germans should treat them with humanity, not because we sought their gratitude or wanted to show how generous of spirit we were, but simply because our experience should have taught us to empathise with human beings in need, regardless of their nationality. At the same time, of course, I believed that those Germans who ordered or committed the crimes the Nazis were responsible for should be punished, but not Germans in general simply because they were Germans. That is when I came to realise that the machine gun I wanted to mount on our balcony when I first arrived in Göttingen was a shameful idea. I concluded that even to contemplate that action reduced me intellectually to the level of those Germans who had killed innocent human beings. What is more, it dishonoured the memory of those who had died in the camps. These early random reflections came over time to solidify into convictions that influenced my thinking and actions in later life.

In 1951, shortly before I left Germany for the United States, Odd Nansen delivered a keynote address at an event organised to coincide with the award of the German Peace Prize to Albert Schweitzer, the famous humanitarian, by the Association of German Booksellers and Publishers. Mutti and I were invited to both events. The Schweitzer ceremony took place in the historic St Paul's church in Frankfurt. I knew, of course, who Schweitzer was and was very moved when Nansen introduced me to him. In his speech Nansen called on the international community to address the plight of German refugees. At the time, the question of whether Germany should be allowed to participate in the 1952 Olympics was still being debated around the world. Nansen urged a favourable decision with the following words: 'It is unjust and senseless to punish the children for the sins of their fathers. But that is what is sought to be done when Germany's young people are kept out of associations [designed to promote] international cooperation.'

The theme of the conference, with its focus on peace and human dignity, had a profound impact on me in terms of the values to which I have devoted much of my life. I still have a dog-eared copy of Nansen's speech and a photograph of Schweitzer holding a little kitten. Taking in the pomp and ceremony which surrounded us in that church – the first such event I had ever attended – I turned to Mutti and whispered, 'Who would ever have thought that we would be allowed into this historic cathedral? Not all that long ago we were *Untermenschen* and now we are invited guests. If only Papa could be with us.' Over the years I have thought often of my father when attending similar ceremonies in Germany and Austria. He, who believed that Hitler and the Nazis would sooner or later be defeated, unfortunately never had the satisfaction of seeing that he was right and witnessing the transformation of Germany into a democratic state.

Nansen came to Göttingen before the Frankfurt conference and told Mutti and me that he wanted to write a book about our camp experiences. He had apparently received many letters from readers of his diary, urging him to tell my story in full. We agreed, naturally, and spent a few days answering his questions, though we heard nothing more about the book during the years that followed. Then, nineteen years later, in 1970, Tommy was published in Norway.* He immediately sent me a copy. Nansen explained that the intervening years had been extremely busy ones in his architectural practice and he had had to put the book project aside. But in 1969 illness had forced him into retirement. With time on his hands he went back to

---

*Tommy: En sannferdig fortelling fortalt av Odd Nansen, published in Oslo by Gyldendal Norsk Forlag, 1970.

his notes from our 1951 interview and wrote the book. Nansen died a couple of years later without getting the book published in any other language. Fortunately, I saw Nansen once more before he died in 1973. While attending a human rights conference in Sweden, I decided to change my return flight to the US in order to spend a few days visiting him in Oslo. I did not know that he was so ill and was shocked to find him in such bad health. He brushed my concerns aside, telling me instead that he was delighted that I was involved in human rights work. Of course, he did not want to hear that he more than anyone else was responsible for my chosen career path. I learned later that he was one of the co-founders of UNICEF, the United Nations Children's Fund. That did not really surprise me. After all, I was one of the beneficiaries of his lifelong commitment to helping children in need.

It was not until 1985, my final year as Dean of the American University's Washington College of Law in Washington, DC, that I was finally able to read Tommy. As my office was preparing the programme for the last graduation ceremony I was to preside over as Dean, I was asked by the President of the Law Students Association to permit him during the ceremony to say a few words on behalf of the graduating class. Of course I agreed and, when the time came, I invited him to take the floor. He walked up to the podium, unwrapped a package in a black binder and told the audience that it was the English translation of Tommy. Explaining that Tommy was a book about my experiences during the Second World War, he continued,

'Dean Buergenthal, the graduating class has commissioned this private English translation of *Tommy* as a token of our appreciation for you so that you will finally be able to read the book that tells your story.' When I was handed the translation I just stood there, overwhelmed by emotion and unable to say a word. It was quite a while before I could continue with the ceremony.

During my time in Göttingen Germany underwent dramatic changes, particularly as far as the economic recovery of the country was concerned. The currency reform, which enabled us to exchange our almost worthless Reichsmarks for the new D-Marks, made a great impression on me. Almost overnight, empty shop windows were filled with products I had never seen before. I think it was during that period that I tasted my first orange. As I was eating it, Mutti told me that oranges were full of vitamin C and that, because they were very expensive and still difficult to obtain, they could only be bought when needed to ward off a cold or influenza. It was also about this time that I had my first taste of Coca-Cola. I don't know from whom or where Mutti obtained the bottle, but she told me that she had heard that it was a very special drink that quenched one's thirst with only a few sips, and that I should drink it only when I was especially parched. She then put the bottle into the cupboard – we did not have refrigerators in those days – and there it sat until I came home one day, terribly thirsty after hours of playing soccer. Mutti agreed that the time had come to open the Coke bottle. The more I drank that sweet, luke-warm drink, the thirstier I got. For years afterwards I only had to look at a bottle of Coca-Cola to recall the unpleasant taste of my first sip.

We had many visitors to our home in Göttingen once travel became easier. Some were people we knew from Kielce who had heard through the grapevine where we were. Others were foreign students or professors who came to Göttingen to study. Some stayed in the Fridtjof-Nansen-Haus, which had been founded after the war by Olav Brennhovd, a Norwegian Protes-tant minister who ended up in a Nazi concentration camp for helping to smuggle Jews from Norway to Sweden. He was a friend of Odd Nansen, who introduced us to him. Brennhovd and his wife became close friends and frequently brought greetings from Nansen and other Norwegians who had known me in Sachsenhausen. Another of our early visitors was a young British soldier who came to Göttingen as a war crimes investi-gator. Greville Janner was told about Mutti and me when he asked to be introduced to members of the Jewish community in Göttingen. He soon realised that basically we were the Jewish community. Greville was only a few years older than I. We became good friends and have remained in touch to this day. He served for many years in the House of Commons before being elevated to the House of Lords. Lord Janner of Braun-stone's lifelong efforts on behalf of victims of the Holocaust probably date back to those early days in Göttingen and other German cities where he met many survivors.

The years I spent in Göttingen after the war were very important in helping me cope with my attitude towards Germany and the Germans. Those were not easy years for Mutti or me, and we often envied some of our fellow Kielce survivors who had ended up in Sweden. They did not have to face the economic hardships we faced in post-war Germany, nor did they have to struggle with the emotions we felt when contemplating the possibility that we were living in the midst of our murderers. At the same time, by living in Germany not long after our concentration camp experience, we were forced to confront those emotions in a way that helped Mutti and me gradually overcome our hatred and desire for revenge. Later, in America, I realised that many of my Jewish friends and acquaintances who had come to the United States before the war and thus escaped the Holocaust were much less forgiving than Mutti or I. I doubt that we would have been able to preserve our sanity had we remained consumed by hatred for the rest of our lives. Many of our relatives and friends in America never understood what we meant when we tried to explain that, while it was important not to forget what happened to us in the Holocaust, it was equally important not to hold the descendants of the perpetrators responsible for what had been done to us, otherwise the cycle of hate and violence would never end.

*Chapter 11*

# To America

I arrived in New York on 4 December 1951. The ship that brought me to the United States was an American military transport, the USNS *General A. W. Greely*, one of the many so-called 'liberty boats' that had been mass-produced in the United States during the war. That December date was a fateful one for me. A new life was about to begin, and an old one had been left behind. But I did not know that at the time, for I travelled to America without a clear sense that I would settle there permanently. All I knew was that I wanted to see America – the America of skyscrapers, big cars, Hollywood movies, chewing gum, cowboys and Indians. That was the America we kids in Göttingen imagined as we tried to find barbers who knew how to give American crew cuts, which had become all the rage in my school. Of course, I looked forward to meeting my uncle and aunt, Eric and Senta Silbergleit – in America the name had become Silberg – and their daughter Gay. I was to live with them in Paterson, New Jersey, less than an hour from New York

Senta and Eric Silberg (formerly Silbergleit),
Thomas's aunt and uncle, 1978

City. The very thought of being so close to Manhattan, Broadway and the hundreds of movie houses I had heard about was all very exciting.

But those were by no means my only reasons for deciding to go to the United States. By 1951, at the age of seventeen, I was beginning to have second thoughts about remaining in Germany for the rest of my life. Although I was quite happy in Göttingen, I came to realise that I never really considered myself to be German the way my classmates, for example, did. The term *Vaterland*, which for the vast majority of Germans evokes patriotic emotions, triggered in me memories of Hitler and the Nazis; so, too, did the sound and words of the German national anthem. I was unable to shed these emotional associations, despite the fact that I was living in a very different Germany, a Germany that was being transformed into a solidly democratic state. These associations served as a constant reminder of the crimes that had been committed in the name of the German *Vaterland*. The fact that I could not disassociate the various nationalistic slogans and symbols from my past set me apart, in my own mind, from ordinary Germans and convinced me that in Germany I would always feel that I was different – different from that mythical 'ordinary German'. That feeling of not belonging, of being different, was, of course, directly related to my past. Moreover, I could still not rid myself entirely of the fear that the world had not seen the last of Nazi Germany. In retrospect, these fears were obviously groundless, but in 1951, when I was seriously beginning to think about my future, only six years had elapsed since the collapse of the Nazi regime and most of us who had survived the camps still could not quite believe that our nightmare was really over. These reflections and doubts about the future convinced me that I would never be able to put my past entirely behind me in Germany and that it would make sense for me to emigrate sooner or later.

I was also forced to think about my future because my uncle and aunt in America kept urging Mutti and me to leave Germany and to settle in the United States. For a variety of reasons Mutti was very reluctant to do so. Her main worry was that she had no profession and that she would not be able to live in America on her German pension. That meant, she believed, that despite her recurring health problems she would have to work in a factory there. I do not know what prompted that idea, although the fact that my uncle and aunt had worked in various factories after they arrived in the US in 1938 may explain Mutti's fear that a similar fate awaited her there. Whatever the reason, she became obsessed with that fear. It may well be that her decision around that time to marry Jacob (Jack) Rosenholz, another Kielce ghetto survivor, was influenced in part by her worries about the life she thought she would have to live in America. She already knew that Jack planned to move to Italy, where he had relatives who wanted him to join them in a business venture.

For me the situation was very different. Although I was eager to accept Uncle Eric and Aunt Senta's invitation to come to America, I did so without committing myself mentally to making it a permanent move. In the back of my mind was the idea that after a year or two in America, I might settle in Israel. There was something romantic about the notion of living in a kibbutz and helping to build a Jewish state. More importantly, while I knew little about the realities of life in Israel, I was sure that I would not feel 'different' there, and that sense of belonging was becoming an important consideration in my thinking about the future. In short, I really did not know what I would or should do in the long term; given my age at the time, the long term seemed very far away. In the meantime, the thought of going to America, whether for ever or only for a year or two, had immense appeal.

My decision to leave Germany for the US was made much easier by Mutti's marriage to Jack Rosenholz and her planned move to Italy with him. Had that not been the case, I would have found it very difficult to leave her alone in Germany. Despite her remarriage, however, it was not easy for Mutti to face another separation from me. Although she agreed that I would have a better future in America and did not try to dissuade me from leaving Germany, she hoped nevertheless that I would be back in Europe within a year or two. At the time, I probably thought the same. Although Mutti and I had many a sleepless night wondering what we should do, some of the problems we worried about, particularly lengthy separations, never materialised. In the years that followed my move to the United States, I managed to visit her almost every second year

*Summer 1951, shortly before the move to the USA*

by getting free rides across the Atlantic on freighters. On these occasions, I also managed to visit my friends in Göttingen.

Mutti had a wonderful life in Italy and was very happy there. And once I completed my studies and then married, Mutti and Jack visited us regularly. These visits became even more frequent after the birth of our sons, when Mutti's previous interest in me shifted dramatically to her grandchildren. Now, as a grandfather myself, I understand that natural process, even though I viewed it with a combination of mild jealousy and a great deal of amusement at the time. I am also very grateful that my sons had the opportunity to get to know their *Oma*, that very special woman.

After various inquiries about the bureaucratic steps necessary for me to enter the United States, I learned that it would make sense for me to seek admission to the country as an immigrant rather than as a visitor or student. It also appeared that I met the requirements to come to America as an immigrant under a special quota for refugee children. In those days, the United States operated a very strict quota system that depended on an applicant's place of birth rather than nationality. Since I was born in Czechoslovakia, I would have fallen under the Czech quota, which had a long waiting list. By contrast, the refugee children's quota was wide open. I applied for a visa under that quota and received it after a brief wait.

A month or two later I was summoned to a transit camp in Bremerhavn, in the north of Germany. I stayed there for about two weeks, undergoing medical tests and interviews by US

*Mutti in Trieste, 1957*

immigration officials. Mutti was with me throughout this time.
She was happy for me, since I was excited about going to
America, but very sad at the thought of not seeing me for so
long. In those days America seemed very far away and I can
only imagine how difficult the idea of my leaving must have
been for her. She kept giving me all kinds of motherly advice:

wear warm clothes in the winter; eat properly, and so on. One tip she gave me still brings a smile to my face: 'Remember, Tommy,' she told me more than once, 'it is better to have many girlfriends than just one. That will ensure that you won't get married too young.' I was never quite able to comply fully with that advice. Mutti had also obtained a fifty-dollar bill on the black market, which was a fortune in those days. She told me to hide it in my shoe so that it would not be confiscated when I arrived. (She must have assumed that they had currency controls in America as they did in Europe at the time.) I did as she said and can now only imagine what that bill must have smelled like after a long voyage aboard a ship whose sanitary conditions left much to be desired. Years later, when I read Emperor Vespasian's famous dictum that money does not smell, I remembered the bill in my shoe. He was certainly wrong about *that* money.

My stay at the transit camp in Bremerhavn was largely uneventful. The camp was filled with refugees from all over Europe. Among them were large numbers of peasants and labourers from eastern Europe and the Soviet Union, many of whom had been brought to Germany as slave labour or prisoners of war. I later learned that this group quite probably included Nazi collaborators who had served as policemen and camp guards during the war and were now claiming refugee status. Another group consisted of those fleeing various eastern European countries that had been taken over by the Soviets. Many of these people were professionals, including lawyers, professors, teachers and medical doctors. Since I spoke German, Polish and schoolboy English, I was called from time to time to act as interpreter for the interviews US immigration examiners conducted with prospective immigrants. It did not take me long to realise that it was quite easy for those who claimed to be peasants and labourers to pass whatever test the examiners were using for admission to the United States. Those refugees who had left their countries for political reasons and were on the whole more educated were asked detailed questions about their background and political views. Judging by the questions the examiners kept asking, I soon realised that they were not really interested in finding out whether or not some of these prospective immigrants had been Nazi collaborators. They focused instead on ascertaining whether they were communists or had leftist leanings. It was only later that I learned that in the early 1950s, when the Cold War was heating up and McCarthyism was at its zenith, the United States had admitted thousands of immigrants from eastern Europe, among them many who had collaborated with the Nazi occupation forces. Years later, when the US government began to deport immigrants who had been found to have committed war crimes during the Nazi period, it was discovered that some of these people had managed to enter the US because of sloppy screening by immigration authorities. I was not surprised.

The voyage to the United States took about ten days. I recently found among my papers a 'Souvenir Edition of the

Greely News', our ship's mimeographed newsletter. From it I learned that there were 1,271 refugees on board the *General Greely*. They were born in twenty countries and professed ten different religions. Roman Catholics constituted the largest religious group with 743 individuals, Baptists the smallest with two. There were fifty Jews on board, sixteen Buddhists and eight Muslims; the remaining passengers represented various other Christian denominations. In many ways the passengers on my ship mirrored the immigration into the US after the war. I had never seen people from so many different countries in one place. I saw many faces whose national or ethnic origins I had not encountered before, and took lots of photographs. I was particularly fascinated by a Kalmyk family, who looked Chinese to me but spoke Russian. They came from the Asian part of the Soviet Union and were, like me, planning to live with relatives in New Jersey. I never did find out how they ended up in Germany.

We slept in single four-tiered bunks on the lower decks of the ship. The distance between the tiers was quite small, making it very difficult to sit up in bed. As soon as we arrived on board we were informed that we were all expected to work, washing the decks, cleaning toilets, painting walls, and so on. I decided right away that there had to be more interesting jobs to perform and that I should try to find myself a more exciting assignment. When I heard that information announcements were frequently being made in different languages over the ship's public address system, I volunteered for that job and was hired for the German and Polish messages. It turned out that I could also serve as one of the German-language editors of the ship's newsletter. With my two assignments came the right to work on the top deck in a very pleasant set of cabins. Since the ship's public address system was located on the bridge, I was also allowed to enter that part of the vessel, which was off-limits to the other passengers. Once they got to know me, the captain and the duty officers let me linger on the bridge after I had made my announcements and patiently answered my many questions about the navigational instruments they used. Captain Niels H. Olsen, the ship's master, told me proudly that he had come to America from Denmark as a young man without a word of English and that life had been good to him in his adoptive country. He assured me that I would be equally happy and successful there.

I owe my introduction to American food to the chefs of the *General Greely*. Our meals were served in the mess hall on long elevated metal tables. We ate our food standing up and had to hold on to our trays whenever the ship listed to one side or the other. In rough seas, the trays of inattentive passengers would end up with a big crash on the other side of the hall. Our typical American breakfast consisted of ham and eggs, milk, coffee and a small box of cereal. The cereal presented a problem for me and many others, for we had no idea what it was or how it was to be eaten. I finally decided that it was some sort of American dessert and carried the cereal box with me to the top deck, where I ate it like candy. I was by no means the only one who laboured under this misconception, for the decks were usually full of passengers eating the dry cereal with their fingers once breakfast was over. Sometimes we were given turkey for lunch or dinner. It was usually served with what I thought were carrots, my favourite vegetable. Never having eaten sweet potatoes before, I could barely swallow my first ever mouthful. Not only did it not taste of carrot, it also reminded me of the turnips I had promised myself never to eat again if I survived the war. In time I came to enjoy sweet potatoes at Christmas and Thanksgiving. On those occasions, however, they are prepared much more appetisingly than those the ship's chefs served us.

Our ship docked in New York harbour during the evening of 3 December 1951. We had to remain on board until the next morning. The New York skyline was ablaze with multicoloured lights. On our way in we passed the fully illuminated Statue of Liberty, which to this day symbolises for me the warm welcome with which America received me as an immigrant. New York City at night is always a special experience, no matter how often you have seen it. But to view it for the first time after leaving a gloomy Europe still recovering from the devastation of a world war was truly a breathtaking experience. I will never forget that moment. As I looked out on that vast city glittering with millions of lights, many thoughts and images raced through my mind. I thought of that recurrent dream I had had in Sachsenhausen that an Allied bomber would lift up my barrack on a big hook and take me to America. That dream had finally come true, albeit not in such a fairy-tale way. I also wondered, not without some trepidation, what life would be like in America, when I would see Mutti again and whether I had done the right thing by leaving Göttingen. But as I stood at the ship's railing, fascinated by a sky drenched in the reflected colours of the myriad lights that illuminated the city, I was transported back to Auschwitz and the reddish-brown smoke bellowing from the crematorium chimneys. Suddenly, the life I had lived – Kielce, Auschwitz, the Death March, Sachsenhausen – flashed before my eyes. Right then and there I knew that I would never quite liberate myself from that past and that it would forever shape my life. But I also knew that I would not permit it to have a debilitating or destructive effect on the new life I was about to begin. My past would inspire my future and give it meaning.

# Epilogue

In the six decades since the end of the Second World War and my liberation, I have often wondered why or how I managed to survive the camps. These reflections are not brought on by feelings of remorse that I survived while so many others did not. Rather, my focus has been on the circumstances that allowed me to survive. If there is one word that captures the conclusion to which I always returned, it is luck. But luck is only the shorthand expression for a combination of factors that allowed me to make it. There was first the fact that during the ghetto and work-camp periods in Kielce I was with my mother and father, who not only cared for me but engrained in me the essentials of survival. Early on in Auschwitz, after I had already been separated from my mother, my father and I were still together. That allowed him to continue to protect me and to instruct me on ways to avoid ending up in the gas chamber. Of course, the fact that I was able to enter Auschwitz without being subjected to the deadly selection process on arrival was a major piece of luck. Had there been a selection, I would never have made it into the camp, and that would have been the end of my story.

*Back in Auschwitz-Birkenau fifty-five years after the Death March*

Once I was alone in Auschwitz, and later on in Sachsen-hausen, it helped that by then I was a little older and had become a true child of the camps in the sense that I had learned the tricks I needed to survive. I use the phrase 'child of the camps' advisedly, because I have always felt that in many ways my survival instincts had much in common with similar traits I have observed in the street children of Latin America, who daily face many dangers and deprivations. These kids are frequently as young as I was, or even younger. I point to these children when friends express surprise on learning how young I was. Children, even relatively young children, learn to be cunning or street smart when circumstances demand, and they are fast learners when they have to be in order to live another day. When my own children were of the age I was during the war, I frequently wondered whether these pampered American kids or those of my friends could have survived in circumstances similar to mine. I am convinced that with some luck they could have, because the survival instinct in children is strong enough to allow them to adjust to the needs of their environment. Of course, what helped me was that I had a relatively long period of survival training. Who knows whether I would have lived had I arrived in Auschwitz from a normal middle-class environment and immediately had to face the brutal camp conditions. It was luck again that I had a gradual immersion into hell. (As I write these words I am not unaware how bizarre it is to use the word 'luck' to describe such circumstances, but that is what it was, in its context.)

I suppose it also helped my chances that I spoke fluent, unaccented German and Polish, and did not look Jewish. My German was useful on a number of occasions, as were my Aryan features; at least, that is what I believe. Maybe I reminded some of the Nazi officers of their own children. This may have been a factor in the decision of the camp commandant of Kielce to let me live after I told him that I could work. Being able to speak Polish also proved useful on numerous occasions. These things no doubt aided my survival yet were entirely fortuitous.

At times I have been asked whether I ever suffered from the so-called 'survivor syndrome' that allegedly afflicts some who torment themselves for surviving when so many others, particularly members of their families, did not. Survivor syndrome has driven some people to suicide and left others with serious psychological problems. I have never experienced such feelings. I don't know why, but if I were to speculate I would attribute their absence to the instinctive belief of children in their immortality and their entitlement to live. It may also be that, since I attributed my survival to sheer luck, I came to view survival and non-survival as a game of chance over which I had no control and therefore bore no responsibility for the outcome. How else to explain the fact that I did not catch diphtheria, even though I slept in the same bunk as my friend who came down with that very contagious disease? It could be argued, of course, that my reliance on luck to explain my survival is itself a defence mechanism against the mental ravages of survivor syndrome. And yet it is no doubt true that luck had a great deal to do with my survival.

I have also wondered from time to time why I can speak and write very freely and, on the whole, unemotionally about my camp experiences, while I am unable to watch movies about the Holocaust or read books that deal with it. That is not to say that writing this memoir was an unemotional experience. There were several moments when I had to compose myself before going on, for example when describing the reunion with my mother or the killing of Ucek and Zarenka. On the whole, however, the story just flowed out of me. And though I had been afraid that some of my Auschwitz nightmares might return as I began to recall seemingly long-forgotten episodes, that did not happen. By contrast, when my children asked my mother to write down some of her Holocaust experiences, she tried, but had to stop after a few pages. She told them afterwards that almost as soon as she began to write she had started to cry and could not continue. Yet she could speak about these events quite freely. How to explain these quirks of the mind? Of course, the Holocaust robbed her of the best years of her life, and while she lived in relative comfort after the war, it certainly was not the normal happy life she might otherwise have had or expected. As she began to write down her war experiences for her grandchildren, the suppressed feelings about her loss no doubt re-emerged. My own past did not really affect my future in the same way.

Nevertheless, my camp experience has certainly shaped my later professional life. Unlike most of my law-school classmates, I was never much interested in the traditional practice of law, that is, in doing what lawyers usually do: defending or prosecuting criminals, representing clients in civil disputes, dealing with family matters or providing a legal consultancy service. Instead, I was drawn to international law, and to international human rights law in particular, because I believed, somewhat naively at first, that these areas of the law, if developed and strengthened, could spare future generations the type of terrible human tragedies that Nazi Germany had visited on the world.

Over time I also gradually concluded that I had an obligation to devote my professional activities to the international protection of human rights. This sense of obligation had its source in the belief, which grew stronger as the years passed, that those of us who survived the Holocaust owe it to those who perished in it to try to improve, each in our own way, the lives of others. To me that meant working towards a world in which the rights and dignity of human beings everywhere would be protected. I also convinced myself that international human rights was the branch of the law to which I, as a lawyer and because of my Holocaust experience, would be able to make the most significant contribution. After all, I knew what it meant to be a victim of human rights violations.

That my Holocaust experience is never entirely separated from my professional work was brought home to me while dealing with a complaint submitted to the UN Human Rights Committee, on which I began to serve in 1995, by the French Holocaust denier Robert Faurisson. Having been convicted in France, where Holocaust denial is a criminal offence, Faurisson challenged both his conviction and the French law. Given my personal history, I decided to remove myself from hearing the case. I did so with the following declaration: 'As a survivor of the concentration camps of Auschwitz and Sachsenhausen whose father, maternal grandparents and many other family members were killed in the Nazi Holocaust, I have no choice but to recuse myself from participating in the decision of this case.'

Before joining the Human Rights Committee I had served on two major international human rights bodies: the Inter-American Court of Human Rights and the UN Truth Commission for El Salvador. In many ways these were my most exciting and productive human rights activities. I was elected as a judge of the newly created Inter-American Court of Human Rights of the Organization of American States in 1979. I remained on the Court, a part-time institution modelled on the old European Court of Human Rights, for the maximum two six-year terms and served as its President for the usual two-year period.

During my time on the Court, much of Latin America was ruled by military regimes and civilian dictators who were responsible for large-scale violations of human rights. While this was not a political climate in which a human rights court could count on the sympathetic support of many governments in the region, the Court was nevertheless able to lay a relatively solid foundation for the enforcement in the western hemisphere of the rights guaranteed by the American Convention on Human Rights. Our most important achievement during my time on the Court was the first ever international judgment holding a state – Honduras – liable for practising a policy of forced disappearances. The government of Honduras was ordered to pay damages to the families of the victims and, what is more, it fully complied with the judgment.

The Court's authority had been severely tested, however, in dealing with the Honduran disappearance cases. After testifying against the government, our first witness was murdered on a street of his home town in Honduras. Another potential witness died in similar circumstances before he ever had a chance to testify. To our relief, the killings stopped as soon as the

Court issued an injunction making the government of Honduras responsible for the safety of our witnesses, potential witnesses and the next of kin of the victims of the disappearances. Our concern that the killing of witnesses would continue despite the injunction, with the government denying all responsibility, proved not to be justified.

Among the court's achievements during that period were important decisions relating to freedom of speech, the protection of human rights during national emergencies, due process of law and related subjects. All in all, because of my interest in strengthening the development of international human rights law and institutions, I found my service on the Inter-American Court to be a dream come true. It is one thing to theorise about solutions to these problems, but quite another to achieve concrete results that strengthen the protection of human rights.

The role that the Inter-American Court could play at the time was severely limited by the fact that some of the most serious violators of human rights in the region – among them Chile, Argentina, Uruguay, Paraguay and various Central American countries – had either not ratified the American Convention or had not accepted the jurisdiction of the Court. These states could consequently not be brought before us. Thus, while we could hear charges against the government of Honduras, which was alleged to have been responsible for some two hundred forced disappearances, we lacked that power for Argentina's military junta, which, it was claimed, was responsible for up to thirty thousand disappearances during its so-called 'dirty war' of 1976–83. The fact that international human rights courts, international criminal courts and similar bodies have jurisdiction only over those states willing to accept it means that states that have not done so enjoy the very impunity these tribunals are designed to end. Sad, but unfortunately true. That is why it is so important, in my opinion, that all states become parties to the Rome Treaty establishing the International Criminal Court, and why I believe that the US should ratify it. By not joining, the US government is sending the wrong message to the international community about its commitment to the international rule of law.

As my service as a judge on the Inter-American Court of Human Rights was coming to an end, the Secretary General of the United Nations appointed me to the three-member United Nations Truth Commission for El Salvador. Our remit was to investigate the massive violations of human rights that had been committed during El Salvador's twelve-year civil war, which had finally ended a few months earlier. Until then I had always believed that my Holocaust experience had hardened me to even the most egregious violations of human rights. In El Salvador I found this not to be true. To see the skeleton of a baby still in the womb of a mother killed in the El Mozote massacre, where around five hundred women, children and old men had been murdered, was more than I could take without being deeply affected by the utter depravity of those who committed such crimes.

On entering the corridor of the residence of a group of Jesuit priests in San Salvador, I was shown the portrait of Archbishop Romero with a bullet hole in the canvas, near his heart. The shot, which to me appeared to be a symbolic re-enactment of the Archbishop's murder some years earlier, was fired by one of the Salvadorean soldiers who, a few minutes later, went on to execute the priests and their housekeeper in the garden of the residence. The murdered priests' 'crime', I learned later, had been their desire to help negotiate a truce between the military and the guerrillas, something the leadership of the military feared. In El Salvador we heard again and again that 'orders are orders', and when we asked some of the military officers or the guerrilla commanders why they had committed or ordered this or that killing, we were invariably told that it was un *error*, a mistake. Never once during our interrogations did I hear an expression of remorse or an admission of guilt; mistakes yes, guilt no. How on earth can the intentional killing of an innocent human being be written off as a mere 'mistake'?

El Salvador was a country in which many lived in fear. In this atmosphere, the victims or their next of kin often did not dare to speak about what had happened to them. People kept their suffering to themselves, hoping for justice but not really expecting it. For some people, ten years or more had gone by in silence and pent-up anger about the past. Finally someone – the Commission – was listening to them, and the mere fact of telling what had happened was a healing emotional release.

I was surprised to discover that, despite their terrible experiences, most of our witnesses were more interested in recounting their story than in seeking retribution.

One interview among many comes to mind in this connection. It involved two women, one Salvadorean and the other either Swedish or Danish. They had come to the Commission together to tell the story of their children. The son of one of the witnesses and the daughter of the other had met in Europe and had fallen in love. The couple travelled to El Salvador, became involved in leftist political activities and were murdered by the military. Their mothers had not met until they decided to testify before the Truth Commission. They told us that they wanted to honour the memory of their children by telling their story together.

During our work in El Salvador, memories of my own past in another part of the world returned to me over and over again as we interviewed witnesses, heard their stories and inspected the killing fields. The suffering that so many people in that small country had endured during its terrible civil war will remain forever imprinted on my soul. While in El Salvador I often wondered whether the fact that I, with my Holocaust background, was investigating these crimes had some symbolic significance. Was it that these activities and my human rights work generally gave special meaning to my survival or that my survival compelled me, whether I knew it or not, to pursue those activities?

In the late 1990s I found myself serving on the Claims

Resolution Tribunal for Dormant Accounts in Switzerland. The CRT, as this tribunal came to be known, was set up to search for unclaimed Holocaust-related bank accounts and help identify their owners or heirs. As its Vice-Chairman, I had to supervise the CRT's day-to-day operations and to adjudicate claims submitted to us. Reading the claimants' applications and the bank files took me back to the 1930s, when some wealthy European Jews, vaguely sensing the fate that awaited them with the rise of the Nazis, had sought to protect their money in neutral Switzerland. Many of them did not survive the Holocaust. That benefited the Swiss banks, which used the funds for more than half a century without ever accounting or expecting to account for their windfall.

Working with a group of commercial arbitrators from Israel, Switzerland, the United States, the United Kingdom and Belgium, plus a support staff of some twenty young lawyers, we were trying to determine whether the information given to us by individual claimants about deceased account holders matched the information found in the files of the Swiss banks. It was no easy task. Frequently all we had to work with was the name of the account holder and, at most, a home town or profession. While I tried not to let my anger at the conduct of some banks affect the job I had to do, it was not always easy. For example some bank files contained nothing but the name of the account holder, the amount of money remaining in the account, and a notation that all other information had been discarded. Not only did the banks not pay interest, they frequently depleted the accounts entirely by deducting bank fees long after they must have known that the depositors had perished in the Holocaust. There was evidence, moreover, that some banks had told Holocaust survivors seeking information about the bank accounts of relatives that no such account existed in the branch the survivors had identified, when they knew perfectly well that the account in question was held at another branch.

There was always great joy in our offices in Zurich when we were able to connect the account of a Holocaust victim to an heir, but there were also moments of sadness when we learned that an heir had died before we had been able to make a finding of entitlement. Many heirs were never found. A case I cannot forget concerned an account claimed by a man and a woman in their seventies, living in different countries, who each contended that they were the sole heir of the account holder. After reviewing the case file, one of our young lawyers came to see me. He reported that the two claimants appeared to be siblings, and that each believed that the other had perished in the Holocaust. I examined the file and agreed with him. The entire office was alerted and there was rejoicing all round: we had not only found the heirs to an account but would also be able to reunite a brother and sister! Because of the claimants' advanced age we decided that the good news should be conveyed to them very carefully and that the brother should be contacted first. When I saw the face of the young lawyer shortly after he had made the call, I could guess what had happened: the brother had died three months earlier without ever learning that his sister was alive.

As Chairman of the Committee on Conscience of the Washington-based US Holocaust Memorial Council, it was my task to relate the experience of the Holocaust to contemporary realities by warning against new genocides and crimes against humanity. By the mid 1990s our optimistic assumption that the world had seen the end of such crimes was belied by what was happening in Rwanda and in the Balkans. Before we had a chance to speak out and get the international community to act, hundreds of thousands had died. That was a familiar story to those of us who had survived the Holocaust. Although we worked very hard to get the international community to take action, it often came too late, if at all, which only went to prove that we are still far from the day when 'Never again!' really means what it is supposed to mean.

Over the years, contemporary events have triggered mental images of my camp experiences. During the Balkan conflict in the 1990s, for example, it was common for TV stations to broadcast pictures of columns of exhausted refugees fleeing from combat zones. As I watched these scenes I recognised myself in the frightened faces of the children. The pictures brought back memories of approaching German tanks on those Polish country roads, where our little group of refugees huddled in fear. When listening to the sole survivor of the El Mozote massacre, I was transported back to the liquidation of the Ghetto of Kielce and the shooting and screams that engulfed us as the sick and infirm were being murdered. In El Salvador, in the courtyard of the residence where the Jesuit priests had been executed, a group of rose bushes planted in their memory obscured the view of a distant observation tower I needed to see. As I tried to look through the rose bushes they gave way in my mind to the images of the beautiful wild flowers I had seen a year earlier on a visit to Auschwitz. They covered the once barren ground of the camp as if to hide the horrendous crimes that had been committed there, just as the roses in that Salvadorean courtyard seemed intent on covering up the murders of the innocent priests. A few years earlier in San José, Costa Rica, I had had a somewhat similar experience while hearing testimony being presented to the Inter-American Court of Human Rights about the tortures and killings that had been committed in Honduras in connection with forced disappearances. As I listened to the witness, I found myself remembering the brutal beating of Spiegel in that barrack in Auschwitz, the killing of the young Poles who had been caught looting during the liquidation of the Ghetto of Kielce, and the beating and subsequent hanging of the prisoners who had tried to escape from the Henryków work camp.

These and similar experiences have frequently accompanied me in my human rights activities. They have forced me to reflect on what it is that allows or compels human beings to commit such cruel and brutal crimes. It frightens me terribly that the individuals responsible for the acts are for the most part not sadists, but ordinary people who go home in the evening to their families, washing their hands before sitting down to dinner, as if what they had been doing all day was just a job like any other. If we humans can so easily wash the blood of our fellow humans from our hands, then what hope is there that future generations will be spared a repeat of the mass killings of the past? Was the Holocaust merely a practice run for the next set of genocides of other groups of human beings? Of course, I am very troubled by these questions, especially when I hear of new atrocities being committed in one part of the world or another.

Such reflections could well have made me a cynic, or caused me to abandon my human rights work. But they have not. For while I do not believe that I survived the Holocaust only in order to devote my life to the protection of human rights, I do believe that, having survived, I have an obligation to try to do all I can to spare others, wherever they might be, from suffering a similar or worse fate. The terrible crimes and cruelties inflicted in many parts of the world since the Holocaust have not weakened my commitment to human rights one jot; instead, they have reinforced my belief in the need to work ever harder to promote human rights education on all levels and to build an international and national legal and political framework that will make governmental violation of human rights increasingly difficult.

It would be a mistake to assume that no significant progress has been made since the Holocaust in protecting human rights. The large body of international human rights laws in existence today, and the many institutions established to enforce them, while they have certainly not put an end to all genocides or crimes against humanity, have certainly prevented or reduced large-scale human rights violations in many parts of the world. Think, for example, of the end of apartheid in South Africa and the emergence of democratic regimes in Latin America and elsewhere. The demise of the Soviet Union with its gulags is, in part at least, attributable to widespread international efforts to put an end to that repressive regime. And who would have dared to dream in the 1970s or 80s that eastern Europe would now be part of a democratic continent? Admittedly, much still remains to be done, but the fact that some progress, however slow, has been made suggests to me that to give up hope now on efforts to improve the human rights situation around the world will only increase the suffering of an ever greater number of human beings and leave them with no prospect of a better future.

I tend to believe that had today's international human rights mechanisms and norms existed in the 1930s, many of the lives that were lost in the Holocaust might well have been saved. The vast numbers of United Nations and regional human rights treaties, declarations and institutions have created an international climate that expects governments to protect human rights and has made it increasingly difficult for them to defend policies that result in serious violations. These laws and institutions have in turn contributed to the growth of non-governmental human rights organisations that alert the international community to serious human rights violations almost as soon as they occur. Some democratic governments have also developed national policies and practices that promote human rights on the international plane. All these efforts have been helped by the contemporary communications revolution, which permits news of human rights abuses and unattended natural catastrophes to be broadcast around the world in almost real time. Mankind's yearning for human rights and human dignity has benefited from political and technological developments that gradually rob offending governments of the legitimacy and support they need to persist over the long run in violating human rights. That we can point to this or that government impervious to these developments proves no more than that progress is slow; it is equally true, though, that the number of such governments is decreasing, if only because in today's world they frequently pay a heavy political and economic price for engaging in practices unacceptable to the wider international community.

None of the international human rights norms, mechanisms or policies to which I have referred existed in the 1930s. The international law of that period allowed governments almost unlimited freedom to mistreat their own citizens. Non-intervention in the internal affairs of a state was the watchword of the day. It not only protected offending governments against international pressure, but also provided other governments with an excuse for inaction. There were few international non-governmental organisations in existence at the time, and the world's media of the day were neither equipped nor interested in stigmatising violations of human rights. Today it is much easier than it was in the 1930s to arouse the international community to action. That does not mean that such action will always be forthcoming, but it does mean that we now have better tools with which to counter large-scale violations of human rights. The task ahead is to strengthen these tools, not to despair, and never to accept that mankind is incapable of creating a world in which our grandchildren and their descendants can live in peace and enjoy the human rights that were denied to so many of my generation.

# Afterword

It took almost seventy years after the end of the Second World War for me to learn the moving details of my mother's search for me after her liberation from Ravensbrück, as well as the events that led up to my father's death in Buchenwald. I obtained this information from documents that were made available to me by the International Tracing Service (ITS) and the Washington-based United States Holocaust Memorial Museum after the publication of this book. As soon as I read these documents, I knew that I had to report what I had found, if only to help bring closure to my family's Holocaust history. This Afterword attempts to do just that.

The ITS is located in Bad Arolsen, a small town in Germany. Housed there are millions of Holocaust-related documents that were recovered from German concentration camp archives and other sources after the war. The ITS also has extensive document holdings that deal with the lives of Displaced Persons (DPs) and concentration camp survivors in the immediate post-war period. I discovered the information about my father's fate in its Holocaust-related document holdings and papers dealing with my mother's search for me in its post-war material.

In documenting the crimes that were committed during the Holocaust and the suffering of its victims, the ITS is an archive like no other. Until the end of 2012, it was administered by the International Committee of the Red Cross under the overall supervision of a council composed of eleven countries, among them the United States, the United Kingdom, France, Russia and Germany. For more than sixty years, these documents were not generally accessible, not to survivors nor to the relatives of those who perished in the Holocaust and who sought information about the fate of their loved ones. As a consequence, my mother, who died in 1991, was never able to find out when, where, or how her husband, my father, died. By the time this cruel and inexcusable policy was reversed, most Holocaust survivors had died.

## Reunion with Mutti

My father, mother and I arrived in Auschwitz-Birkenau on 2 August, 1944. My father and I were separated from Mutti upon our arrival at the Birkenau railroad ramp. Mutti was taken to one of the women's camps, while my father and I ended up in the so-called Gypsy Camp, named for the Roma and Sinti families who had been held there until they were all murdered shortly before our arrival. I saw Mutti in Auschwitz only once, for a brief moment, across the barbed wire separating her camp from the others. I did not see her again until we were reunited in December 1946.

In October or November 1944, Mutti was sent from Auschwitz to Ravensbrück, a concentration camp for women near Berlin. She was moved from there to Malchow, a sub-camp of Ravensbrück, where some 5,000 women were forced to work under terrible conditions. In late April 1945, as Soviet troops approached, Malchow's SS guards abandoned the camp and marched its inmates in the direction of another camp further away from the Front. Before Mutti and her fellow prisoners reached that destination, they were liberated by Soviet troops, less than two weeks before the end of the war in Europe. Emaciated from months of hard labour, hunger and the long march, Mutti and a group of her friends lived for a few days in empty houses from which their German owners had fled to avoid falling into Soviet hands. Many of these houses were stocked with food Mutti had not seen in years; there she could sleep in a real bed with blankets and pillows and soak in a bath, all luxuries she had given up hope of ever enjoying again. The temptation to remain longer in one of these houses was great, but she knew that for her the war would not be over until she found my father and me.

Before they were separated, my parents had agreed on the places they would look for each other if they survived the war. Among the towns on their list were Kielce in Poland, where we had been in the Ghetto, and my mother's hometown, Göttingen in Germany. As soon as she felt strong enough to embark on the search, Mutti looked for a way to get to Kielce. That was by no means easy. She had no passport, documents or money.

And travel from Germany to Poland in the chaos that engulfed Germany in the days following its surrender was difficult and at times dangerous. Very few trains moved along the railroad tracks that had not been bombed, and those that did were almost all reserved for the military personnel of the Occupying Powers. The roads were clogged with refugees, camp survivors, Soviet and Polish military vehicles, trucks and cars seized from their German owners by ex-prisoners of war and slave labourers trying to return to their homes in Eastern Europe. Although she understood Polish, Mutti spoke only German and therefore ran the risk of being taken for a German. That is why, when asked what her nationality was, she would claim to be Hungarian. But since she spoke no Hungarian either, she was always in fear of running into Hungarian-speakers.

At times on foot, sometimes hitchhiking, it took Mutti a couple of weeks to reach Kielce. There she was warmly welcomed by other Kielce Ghetto survivors who had already established a rudimentary Jewish community organisation to help returning 'Kielcers' with food and housing. Most important for all of them, of course, was information about their missing relatives. 'Had they survived?' or 'Where had they been seen last?' were the questions most frequently asked. Mutti asked about my father and me. Some survivors told her that they had seen both of us in Auschwitz; others were sure that my father had been sent to Flossenbürg; and a few claimed to know that he had been executed or died there. As for me, one or two survivors told Mutti that they thought they had seen me in

Sachsenhausen or on the death march out of Auschwitz. No one seemed to have seen me after the war. Mutti was frequently reminded that almost all Jewish children – many older than I – had been murdered, making it unlikely that I had survived. Some old friends among the returnees tried gently to convince her that I could not possibly be alive. 'Stop torturing yourself, Gerda,' they would say, 'Think of your health.'

That was advice Mutti was not ready to accept. After all, had not the fortuneteller told her that I was a 'lucky child'? I had to be alive; it could not be otherwise. At the same time, though, she was increasingly less certain of my father's survival because of the rumours she kept hearing that all inmates of the Flossenbürg concentration camp had been executed shortly before the end of the war. Despite all that Mutti had learned in Kielce, she knew that her search had to continue, and this time from Göttingen.

Her return trip to Germany was no less difficult or strenuous than her trip to Kielce. Mutti probably arrived in Göttingen in early June 1945. Exhausted and in need of medical treatment, she admitted herself to the town's university clinic. As soon as she regained her strength, Mutti renewed her search for us. Not finding my father or any news of him in Göttingen, Mutti was forced to conclude, without as yet giving up all hope, that it was most unlikely that my father had survived.

On 13 July, 1945, Mutti stumbled on some very exciting news. While reading a German newspaper that also served as the bulletin of the Occupation Powers, she saw a photograph

Document 1

of a British soldier crossing a street in Berlin with five children, all about my age (Document 1). The longer she looked at it, the more she convinced herself that I was the second child from the right in that picture. Here, finally, was the confirmation she had awaited so long: I had survived the war! Now all that remained was to find me.

As a matter of fact, I was not the child in the newspaper picture, though Mutti had no doubt whatsoever that it was me. That was all that mattered to her: the photograph energised her search and helped her to convince others that I was alive.

Shortly after her arrival in Göttingen, an American search organisation had helped Mutti locate her brother Eric and his wife Senta. Eric and Senta Silberg, formerly Silbergleit, had emigrated to the US from Germany in 1938. Senta's brother, Freddy Marling, formerly Markstein, had fled to Britain at about the same time. While serving in the British army, Freddy had learned from Senta that Mutti was alive and living in Göttingen, which was in the British Zone of Germany. Immediately he decided to visit her and by sheer chance reached Göttingen at about the time Mutti had discovered the Berlin photograph. As soon as Mutti showed it to him, Freddy asked the British military authorities in Germany to assist in finding the British soldier in that photograph. The search for me had now begun in earnest. As early as 17 July, 1945, British military authorities addressed the following communication (Document 2) to their Displaced Persons Office, again attaching a copy of the photograph:

```
SUBJECT:-   Missing Relatives - DPs.                326MG/10/48.

TO:-        DP Det Control HQ, Wunstorf.

FROM:-      OC 326 (R) Det Mil Gov.

------------------------------------------------


              Tommy BURGENTHAL.  (German Jew)

          May efforts please be made to trace the where-abouts
of the a/m.

          A photo of the boy, recently taken in BERLIN, appeared
in a copy of the Hanover Courier (enclosed herewith), and his
mother, GERDA BURGENTHAL residing at Gauss-Str. 4 aI, GOTTINGEN,
wishes to trace him.

          The boy is marked with a cross in the enclosed picture.
He was formerly in a Concentration Camp at ORANIENBURG.



                                    ?????????????????
                                                    Major.
In the Field                        Commanding 326(R) Det Mil Gov.
17 Jul 45
DHM/LA
```

In the United States the Silbergs appealed to various American search organisations for help in locating me, their nephew. These organisations mounted a massive search effort that in time involved the American Joint Distribution Committee, the United Nations Relief and Rehabilitation Administration (UNRRA), Red Cross Societies in various countries, the Jewish Agency for Palestine, as it was then known, and a number of foreign governments. The existence of the photograph proved to be vital. It helped dispel the argument Mutti frequently had to contend with, that I could not possibly be alive because so few children my age had survived the camps. At the same time, though, the search kept focusing on false clues leading in wrong directions. For example, on 21 January, 1946, the Search Bureau of the Control Commission for Germany issued an 'Enquiry Concerning Missing Person' with the following information about me: 'Mother has seen photo of her son in *Hannoverscher Kurier* dated 13 July, 45 – crossing street in Berlin with British M.P. and several other boys. One boy, Natek Hochmann, his friend, is known to be in Palestine.'

The reference to Natek Hochmann seemed to suggest that I had also headed to Palestine or was on route there via Italy. Once information had been received confirming that I was not in Palestine, on 28 May, 1946 the UNRRA Tracing Bureau in Germany asked its Italian headquarters for information about me, explaining that I 'probably went to Milan, Italy.' Many illegal transports to Palestine went through Milan in those days, leading the letter writer to assume that I might still be in Italy, possibly because I had become sick while on route to Palestine.

Just how astray the search went from there emerges from a letter, dated 6 July, 1946, prepared by the same UNRRA office. It refers to information provided by the Jewish Agency suggesting that I may never have left Berlin or conversely, might have been evacuated from Berlin under some scheme for the protection of children. The brief attached to this letter, entitled 'Action to date,' summarised the result of the search for me between November 1945 and April 1946 as follows (Document 3):

Action to date

| | |
|---|---|
| 8 Nov 45 | Sent to Berlin office. |
| 11 Dec 45 | Nil report submitted by Berlin office. |
| 16 Jan 46 | Mrs Buergenthal interviewed by special Search Officer. |
| 22 Jan 46 | Case sent to Jewish Agency, Palestine for investigation. |
| 30 Jan 46 | Case taken by Special Search Officer Capt ARNON returning to Palestine to be demobilised. |
| 28 Feb 46 | British Red Cross Record Bureau Rome requested by signal to confirm fresh statement from Mother that her son passed through MILAN on way to Palestine last summer. |
| 7 Mar 46 | British Red Cross London requested to confirm news that boy is actually Palestine and to report any further action taken. |
| 18 Mar 46 | Letter from Palestine stating there is no trace of Burgenthal there. But his friend KATEK HOCHMANN traced. |
| 1 Apr 46 | Sent on special Radio List to Hamburg. |
| 1 Apr 46 | British Red Cross in London confirm that Burgenthal is not in Palestine |

The search did not end here. On 22 May, 1946, the director of the Central Tracing Service of the British army notified his military superiors that his office had received a report from Berlin police channels that 'Tommy Burgenthal' could not be located in Berlin and that investigations made at all Berlin police precincts and at the Jewish Community were in vain. And as late as 11 September, 1946, the Geneva-based Jewish Information Centre – the Fichier Central Juif – provided a similar reply to the effect that 'up to date, we have received no information on the whereabouts of the person(s) [Tommy Buergenthal] to be traced on your behalf.'

During all this time, Mutti's initial euphoria gradually turned into desperation and fear. The different organisations looking for me kept her informed that they had not yet found me. Every time one of these letters arrived, she opened it hoping that it would bring the news she was longing for. The longer she had to wait, the more she began to fear the worst. It is ironic that I had in fact been in Berlin, but that was before British and American troops entered the city. I had been with the Scout Company of the Polish Kosciuszko Division, who had adopted me as its mascot shortly after I had been liberated from Sachsenhausen. My company had entered Berlin about the same time as the Soviet troops and had fought alongside them in the Battle of Berlin. After the fall of the city and the subsequent German surrender, we had been ordered to return to Poland, where I had spent a few months with my company in a Polish military garrison in the city of Siedlice. As the Division began to demobilise, a Jewish soldier who had become my friend had placed me in a Jewish orphanage in Otwock, a town close to Warsaw. I arrived in November 1945.

It is therefore not surprising that Mutti and the search organisations helping her could not find me. Thrown off course by the photograph Mutti had provided them, they were looking for me in all the wrong places. Had British or American troops liberated me, the search bureaus they had established in

Germany would probably have located me without much delay because they tried to register all freed camp inmates. That was not true in the territory captured by Soviet and Polish troops.

By the time I arrived in the Otwock orphanage the search for me had focused on the British military, Sachsenhausen, Palestine and Italy, and had proved unsuccessful. The Berlin photograph diversion obviously prolonged the effort to find me, but that photograph was vital in keeping Mutti convinced that I had survived. It also made it morally difficult for the various search agencies to cease looking.

I was found, more than a year and a half after Mutti had begun her search for me and more than two years after we had been separated in Auschwitz. To this day, it is difficult for me to imagine how she must have suffered during this period. She had survived the Ghetto of Kielce, Auschwitz and Ravensbrück; had to accept that my father had not survived; and had reason to believe – thanks to the photograph – that I was alive, yet I was nowhere to be found. Could it be that she was wrong and that the child in the picture was not me? And what if I had died on the Death March out of Auschwitz or later in Sachsenhausen or some other camp? Could I have been adopted and taken to some faraway country? Maybe I had forgotten my name? On and on she tormented herself with these questions, especially when yet another letter arrived informing her that my whereabouts were still unknown. Then she would pull out the photograph once more and reassure herself that I was alive and that she would eventually find me.

How I was found is a fascinating story in itself. The Jewish Bund, a leftist Socialist organisation working in Poland, administered the orphanage in Otwock, and was opposed to Jewish immigration to Palestine. That led a Zionist youth organisation, Hashomer Hatzair, to surreptitiously place one of its members on the staff of the orphanage with the mission of convincing as many children as possible to volunteer to be taken to Palestine. Those who volunteered were told to run away from the orphanage, one at a time, at intervals of a few weeks. They would then be met by a Hashomer representative a few blocks down the road and taken to a makeshift kibbutz in Poland. From there, via Italy by illegal transport, they would eventually reach Palestine.

A few months after I arrived at the orphanage, the Hashomer counsellor, whom I liked very much, approached me with what she called a 'secret between us.' Did I want to leave the orphanage to live in Palestine, she asked me in a conspiratorial tone. I said yes and wanted to know how soon I could leave. She replied that I would have to be the last child to run away because my departure would attract public attention and put an end to the entire operation. As the only child in the orphanage who had survived Auschwitz, I was frequently interviewed by newspaper reporters and introduced to important visitors, and thus I became rather well known. My counsellor promised me that I would not be left behind, that she would ensure my name appeared on the list of the children who wanted to live in Palestine.

She proved to be true to her word. My name was on the list, and that is how it reached the Jewish Agency for Palestine in Jerusalem. Much earlier, through the efforts of Uncle Eric and Aunt Senta in the US, the Jewish Agency had received a number of requests to assist Mutti in finding me. Keep in mind that in those early post-war years, the Agency's offices were flooded with search requests from hundreds of thousands of individuals from many parts of the world. Now, imagine one person sitting at a desk in Jerusalem. As he goes through the many search files assigned to him that day, he comes across the list of children from Otwock who want to go to Palestine. At that point, he remembers that he had seen a search file from a mother looking for her son, whose name appears on that list. As he wades through the earlier files, he finds Mutti's search form and concludes that there can be no doubt that the boy on the Otwock list is her son. To this day, I marvel at the diligence and commitment of the researcher and the sheer luck that led to my being found. And that in an era before computers!

The Jewish Agency must have announced in late August or early September 1946 that it had found me. I was unable to recover a copy of its initial announcement and therefore do not have a precise date, but by the latter part of September organisations were reporting that I had been located. On 24 September, 1946, the Search Bureau of the British Army of the Rhine (BAOR) reported to the Child Welfare Section of UNRRA that 'information has now been received from the Jewish Agency in Palestine that the a/m [Tommy Burgenthal] is living in the

Tel: GOTTINGEN 3040

Ref: PWDP/55700/VIP 180

To: Polish Liaison Officer (Mme Los)
att Central Tracing Bureau
390 UNRRA Central H.Q.,
BAOR.

55 Search Bureau
B.A.O.R.

30 September, 1946

Subject: . Tommy BUERGENTHAL - VIP 180

1. This Bureau has been working for a year on a case for the above named CZECH child, and has recently succeeded in ascertaining his whereabouts.

2. The child is in POLAND at the JEWISH ORPHANAGE in OTWOCK, and can be contacted through the following authorities.

MIEJSCOWY KOMITET ZYTOWSKI
OTWOCK
K.WARSAWY
POLAND.

3. The poor mother is naturally so overcome with the good news that she can scarcely believe that her child has really been found at last and is anxious to receive concrete information from the orphanage.

4. We would be most grateful if you could contact either (a) the Jewish Committee or (b) the orphanage, as quickly as possible and request them to advise us of the child's welfare etc. It may also

/OVER...

be humane to request them to tell the child as they deem best, that his parents are alive and well. He is, however, only 12 years old, but it was considered probable that he was under the impression that they had been killed in AUSCHWITZ.

5. If you could settle this as expeditiously as possible, preferably by telegram it would be much appreciated by this office.

6. Awaiting an early reply from you we offer our grateful thanks for your co-operation and assistance.

(S.MOURANT)
for R.E.H.STOTT
COLONEL
Director of Bureau

SM/GH

Documents 4a and 4b

Jewish Orphanage in Otwock, Poland.' I do not know exactly when Mutti received the news. I assume, though, that it was earlier in September because on 30 September, 1946 the British Army Search Bureau was able to address these communications to the Polish Liaison Officer at the UNRRA Tracing Bureau (Documents 4a and 4b, p. 243).

Then, on 1 October, 1946, the Warsaw office of the American Joint Distribution Committee (the Joint) was requested by its London Headquarters to inform me that 'my parents' had survived the war, that they lived in Göttingen, and that they were trying to bring me to Göttingen. Later that month, the Joint's London office sent the following information it had received from the orphanage about me to its German office, to be provided to Mutti (Document 5, opposite).

Other than the initial news that I had survived the war and was in the Otwock orphanage, this was the first information Mutti received about me. It must have made her very happy, particularly hearing that I was in good health.

Despite the fact that I had been told that 'my parents' were alive, it was only after Mutti and I were reunited that I learned that my father had not survived. While in the Polish army and afterwards in the orphanage, I had always assumed that my parents were alive and would eventually find me. That is why I never sought help to find them. After seeing so many people die in the camps, I still cannot understand how I could have been so sure that my parents had survived the war. Of course, as more and more time passed after my liberation without word from them,

Document 5

I would sometimes wonder why they had not yet found me. Still, I pushed those thoughts out of my mind almost as fast as they arose. Being the child I was, I simply could not admit to myself that my parents might have died like so many others.

I can imagine Mutti's reaction to the news that I was alive: disbelief, tears, excitement for days on end. She was ready to leave for Poland to collect me immediately, but that proved to be impossible. Travel between Germany and Poland was still extremely difficult and required a multitude of documents that took months to obtain, prompting Mutti again to turn to the Joint for help. What she did not know was that the Joint was already hard at work trying to get me to Göttingen. Simultaneously with its letter asking that I be told that my parents were alive, the Joint asked the search bureau of the British Army in Germany to help obtain the information about my parents and me that might be required by the Polish authorities to grant permission for my departure from Poland. In addition to providing the requested information, the search bureau made a special point of noting how widespread its search for me had been. 'This Bureau has been working on this case for a year, and enquiries have been conducted on the highest level in London, Jerusalem, Prague, Berlin, Italy, etc.'

Now the focus shifted to bringing me to Mutti in Göttingen. The same energy and enthusiasm that led to me being found is also reflected in those efforts, spurred on by Mutti's unrelenting pressure to ensure that no time was lost in reuniting us. That did not prove as easy as she had initially assumed it would be. I had no passport, no birth certificate or other documents. Under normal conditions, it would have been reasonable to seek permission from the Polish government to allow me to leave Poland, explaining my family and camp background. But conditions in Poland were by no means normal at the time. The country was still recovering from a disastrous war that had ended a little over a year earlier. That is why the director of the Warsaw office of the Joint decided on a different approach to bring me to Göttingen (Document 6).

AMERICAN JOINT DISTRIBUTION COMMITTEE
POLAND

Warsaw, November 4th, 1946

Secr. 7300
F
:
        American Joint Ditribution Committee
        Mil.Gov. 618
        B.A.O.R.

Re: Tommy Burgenthal

Dear Sirs,

    We received your two letters dated October 16th and 19th. Enclosed you will find a copy of our letter to AJDC.London, from which you will see that Tommy is already informed of his mother's whereabouts and is contacting her directly.-

    In order to reunite mother and child as soon as possible we would suggest you that we should send the child to the border if you could make proper arrangements to take him over and to bring him to his mother.- The easiest way in our opinion would be through AJDC Prague.-

    We should appreciated if you contacted Prague and let us know by your earliest convenience.

    We thank you for your kind cooperation

AMERICAN JOINT DISTRIBUTION
COMMITTEE

William Bein
Director for Poland

1 enclosure

In short, in proposing to 'send the child to the border' and 'bring him to his mother', the director of the Joint's Warsaw office was asking for permission to arrange an illegal border crossing for me.

Unaware of the steps that the Warsaw office had proposed, Mutti was getting more and more concerned about the delay in getting me to Göttingen. This is apparent from the letter that follows (Document 7).

```
Search Bureau                                    November 8, 1946.

To: AJDC Warsaw.  Att. Mr. Bein

Re: Tommy Bürgenthal c/o Otwock Orphanage.

      The mother of the a/n child was just in our office requesting us
to forward to you this enclosure as she fears the Polish Authorities
would not allow the transfer of the child unless it is German.

      We assured the mother, that everything possible will be done on
our side to reunite the child with the legal mother. She showed us the
first letter she received from the child and you will understand how an-
xious she is to have the child at the earliest possible moment.
      We would very much appreciate if you could give this case priority,
so that the poor mother can have her only surviving beloved one at the
earliest possible moment.

      Thank you in advance for your kind co-operation.

                                             Harry Kopp
                                      for Wm. B. Schwartz Zone Directo
```

What Mutti had no way of knowing was that on 26 November, 1946, the various European Joint offices had agreed to make the necessary arrangements to bring me to Göttingen illegally. The procedure that they had decided upon is set out in the following cable (Document 8):

*Sigenthal*
*Tommy*

AMERICAN JOINT DISTRIBUTION COMMITTEE
Headquarters for Germany
c/o UNRRA CHQ                          APO 757

C A B L E

26 November 1946

TO:    JOINTFUND
       PRAGUE

RE TOMMY BUERGENTHAHL AGE TWELVE YEARS CARE OF JEWISH
ORPHANAGE OTWOK POLAND SUBJECT TRANSFER OF ABOVE
NAMED CHILD TO JOIN HIS MOTHER IN BRITISH ZONE GERMANY      STOP
JOINT WARSAW AGREES TO BRING CHILD TO CZECH BORDER
PLEASE CONTACT JOINT WARSAW ABOUT DATE OF CHILD'S
ARRIVAL AT BORDER STOP JOINT BELSEN WILLING TO
PICK UP CHILD IN PRAGUE PLEASE CABLE US IMMEDIATELY
IF YOU AGREEABLE TO BRING CHILD TO PRAGUE AND TO
KEEP IT UNTIL REPRESENTATIVE AJDC BELSEN ARRIVES

                              AJDC BELSEN

                CHARGE TO
                      JOINTFUND
                      FRANKFURT

                (Originating Division:
                      Jointfund Frankfurt (Supply)
                      Room 637    22609

Distribution:  cc Frankfurt office
               ✓ Belsen
               Supply-files

Document 8

By this time, I knew that plans were being made for me to be sent to Germany, but I had no idea how or when I would travel. Whenever I asked the director of the orphanage, and I asked her almost every day, she replied that it would be soon. That was probably all she herself was being told. About a week later, the Joint's Warsaw office cabled its other European offices: 'Tommy Burgenthal leaving for Prague this week.' I must have been told at about the same time to get ready for my departure from the orphanage. I was so excited that I began to pack immediately. The few belongings I had fit into a small rucksack. I was ready to leave in less than an hour but had to wait a few days more before I was picked up from the orphanage.

During the first stage of my trip to Göttingen I was accompanied by a staff member of the Joint, until our train arrived at a small town near the Czech border. Not far from there, I crossed the border with a group of other Jewish camp survivors and two guides who were there waiting for us. The guides advised us that since we had no papers, we would have to cross the Polish–Czech frontier illegally by walking through a nearby forest. We were not running any risks, they assured us, 'Everything is taken care of,' but we must stay with the group and not make any noise because 'One never knows what can happen.'

The border crossing was successful and uneventful, except that, because of the cold and snow (it was December after all), my right foot began to hurt where my toes had been amputated. That made it increasingly difficult for me to walk. On arrival at the Czech side of the border, I was separated from the group I had travelled with and taken to Prague, where I stayed for a few days with a young American woman who was the Joint's representative in that city. She was very kind to me, showed me many interesting sites of this beautiful city, and took me to some fine restaurants because she thought that I needed to gain some weight. My trip from Prague to Göttingen, through the American Zone in Germany to the British Zone where Mutti lived, took a few days more.

About an hour or two before the train arrived in Göttingen, I could no longer remain in my seat. I kept jumping up, leaving the compartment, looking out of the window, and wishing that the train would not make so many stops. When the train finally rolled into the Göttingen station, I saw Mutti nervously scanning the windows of the passing train. As soon as I saw her, and before the train had come to a full stop, I jumped out and raced towards her. We embraced, held each other very tightly with tears in our eyes, and kept asking question after question, trying to make up for the two years during which we had been separated. From time to time Mutti would look at me and touch me as if to assure herself that she was not dreaming, that I was finally in her arms. Then she would kiss me again and again. We remained standing there long after the train had left the station.

After my reunion with Mutti, the Joint, which had played such an important role in helping bring about this wonderful day, issued the following communique (Document 9):

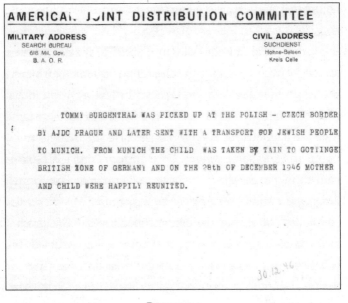

AMERICAN JOINT DISTRIBUTION COMMITTEE

MILITARY ADDRESS
SEARCH BUREAU
618 Mil. Gov.
B. A. O. R.

CIVIL ADDRESS
SUCHDIENST
Hohne-Belsen
Kreis Celle

TOMMY BURGENTHAL WAS PICKED UP AT THE POLISH – CZECH BORDER
BY AJDC PRAGUE AND LATER SENT WITH A TRANSPORT OOF JEWISH PEOPLE
TO MUNICH. FROM MUNICH THE CHILD WAS TAKEN BY TAIN TO GOTTINGE
BRITISH ZONE OF GERMANY AND ON THE 28th OF DECEMBER 1946 MOTHER
AND CHILD WERE HAPPILY REUNITED.

30.12.46

Document 9

Today, in the eightieth year of my life, sixty-eight years after I saw Mutti waiting at the railroad station in Göttingen, and seventy years after we were separated in Auschwitz, I still cannot think of that day without reliving the moment of our miraculous reunion.

## My Father's Last Days

It was not until I was reunited with Mutti at the Göttingen railroad station that I learned that my father had died in the camps. After we kissed and embraced, I asked Mutti 'Und Papa?' She said nothing but started to cry, no longer the happy tears she had shed a moment before, but tears of immense sadness and pain. That is when I knew.

I saw my father for the last time in October 1944 when I was torn away from him during a selection in Birkenau. All I knew about his fate after we were separated I learned from Mutti, when we were reunited in Göttingen. And all she knew came from what some Kielce survivors had told her: that he and a group of other inmates were sent to the concentration camp of Flossenbürg in Germany. Some of these survivors also claimed to know that my father had been executed a few days before the end of the war, together with many of the remaining inmates of that camp. For many years thereafter, I had assumed this information to be correct and so reported it in the different language editions of this book, including its US and UK hardcover editions, which were published in 2009. A year later, by the time the English language paperback editions were ready to go to press, I discovered that my father had actually died in Buchenwald. At that point, I was still able to correct the error that appeared in the earlier editions.

But this was not the whole story. I have since learned, at about the same time I obtained the documents about Mutti from the International Tracing Service in Bad Arolsen, that my father had not been sent directly from Auschwitz to Buchenwald. Instead, after we were separated in Auschwitz, he was taken to Sachsenhausen, arriving there on 26 October, 1944. He remained in Sachsenhausen for about three weeks before being moved again, this time to Buchenwald where he arrived on 13 November, 1944. He died on 15 January, 1945, in Ohrdruf-Nord, a Buchenwald sub-camp. American troops liberated that camp on 2 April, 1945.

Whenever I look at these dates, I keep asking myself: What if Papa had remained in Sachsenhausen and not been moved to Buchenwald? What if he had not died a few short months before the liberation of his camp? Yes, what if ...? I cannot help reflecting on these questions because I had arrived in Sachsenhausen after the Auschwitz Death March early in February 1945. Had my father remained in Sachsenhausen we might have been reunited there. And if he had not died in January 1945, he and I would both have been liberated in April 1945 and reunited with Mutti either in Kielce or Göttingen, probably in May 1945. Then Papa, Mutti and I would have been together again. If only my dreams could have produced that happy ending! But that was not to be.

I found the date of my father's death in a number of Buchenwald documents. There is first his official death certificate, signed by the medical officer of the Ohrdruf-Nord 'command'. It indicates that my father died on the morning of 15 January, 1945; that the cause of death was double pneumonia; and that he was admitted to the infirmary on the previous day (Document 10, opposite).

Yet another document is a handwritten diagnosis of my father's medical condition, which appears to have been prepared at the time of his admission to the infirmary (Document 11, p. 256).

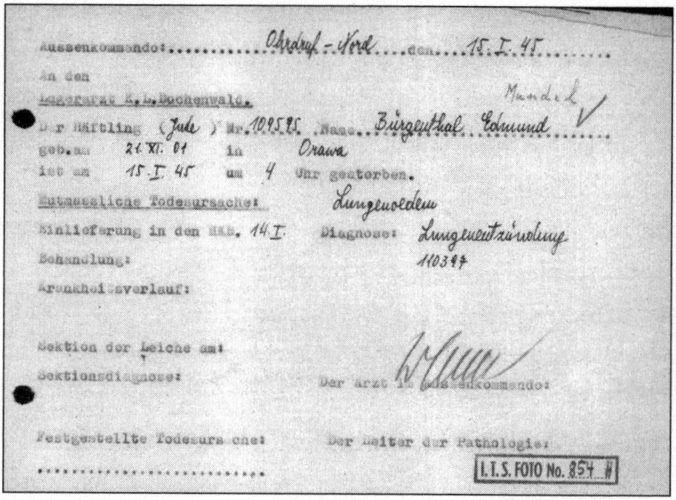

Aussenkommando: Ohrdruf-Nord den 15. I. 45

An den

Lagerarzt K.L. Buchenwald.

Mandel

Der Häftling (Jude) Nr. 109585 Name Bürgenthal Edmund

geb. am 21. XI. 01 in Orawa

ist am 15. I. 45 um 4 Uhr gestorben.

Mutmassliche Todesursache: Lungenoedem

Einlieferung in den HKB. 14. I. Diagnose: Lungenentzündung

Behandlung: 110347

Krankheitsverlauf:

Sektion der Leiche am:

Sektionsdiagnose: Der Arzt im Aussenkommando:

Festgestellte Todesursache: Der Leiter der Pathologie:

I.T.S. FOTO No. 854 II

Document 10

A third document, which I have not reproduced, consists of a single-page temperature chart.

My initial reaction on seeing these documents was disbelief. I had assumed that my father had been executed and that these medical reports were fabrications designed to give the impression that he had died of natural causes. The end of the war and Germany's defeat had been close at that point. That must have been obvious to most Germans at the time. A cover-up was therefore not out of the question, considering that the SS and Gestapo routinely announced that an individual they had executed had been 'killed while trying to escape'. '*Auf der Flucht erschossen*' was the phrase heard frequently on those occasions. However, these documents are much too detailed to

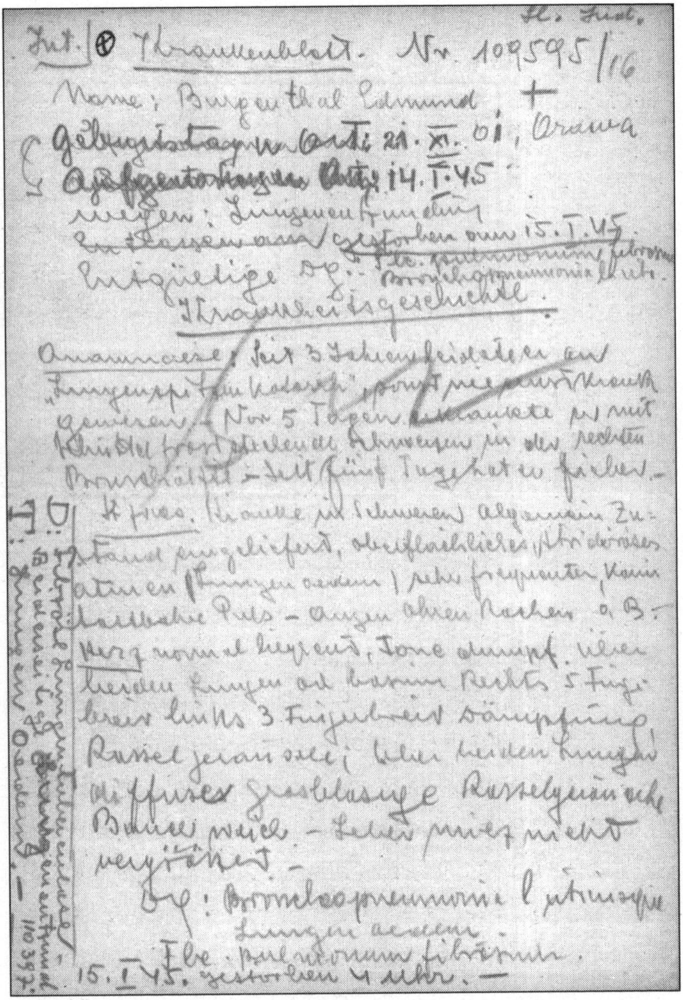

Document 11

justify the conclusion that they were fabrications. After all, my father was not a world famous person whose execution might have justified such a detailed cover-up. It is therefore not unreasonable to accept that the immediate cause of my father's death was indeed double pneumonia. But it is also true that his death, like that of so many others in that camp, was the result of the hunger, hard labour, and lack of warm clothing in the bitter winter of January 1945 to which the inmates of Ohrdruf-Nord were subjected.

I cannot end this Afterword without reproducing my father's camp identity card (Document 12, overleaf). Notwithstanding some erroneous entries regarding my father's nationality and place of birth, this document has a very special meaning for my family and me. It shows that my father was born on 11 November, 1901; that he entered Auschwitz II/Birkenau on 2 August, 1944; that he was sent from there to Sachsenhausen on 26 October, 1944, and then, on 13 November, 1944 to Buchenwald, where he died in the forty-fourth year of his life.

This single piece of paper, found among the millions of document files on deposit in Bad Arolsen, traces the way stations of my father's suffering during the Holocaust: the Ghetto of Kielce, Auschwitz, Sachsenhausen and, finally, Buchenwald, where he died four months before the end of the war. This document is my father's only memorial. There are no others, not even a marked grave with his remains in a cemetery, where my family – my wife and I, our children, grandchildren and their descendants – would be able to express our love and

Document 12

respect for a man who had to die for no reason other than that
a murderous regime decreed that he had no right to live.

## The Other Victims

My father is just one victim among the many millions, Jews and
non-Jews alike, who shared his fate, including my maternal
grandparents who died in Treblinka and many other close relatives. They also have no gravestones and no memorials other than
a mention in one or more Bad Arolsen files. For them, as for my
father, these files serve as the spiritual depositary of their unful-
filled lives, dreams, and hopes. All of them were murdered
because of their religion, race, ethnic identity, sexual orientation
or political views that the Nazis decided had to be eliminated.

Also recorded in Bad Arolsen are my mother's camp history and her post-war search for me. Even though everybody told her that I could not possibly have survived, she believed that I was alive. She persisted in her search. Similar stories abound in these files, a few happy ones, the vast majority not: Think of the many mothers and their children who were not as lucky as my mother and I.

But that is only part of the story. The documents in Bad Arolsen are silent about the loss mankind as a whole has suffered because of the murder of some million Jewish children during the Holocaust. We will never know how many of these children, had they lived, might have earned Nobel Prizes for their contributions to world peace, medicine, physics, literature and so on. Or how many among them might have become distinguished poets and writers, actors, painters, scholars, musicians, architects, engineers, surgeons, scientists and master craftsmen, each making ours a better, more knowing and more beautiful world. That is but one reason why the Holocaust is not only a Jewish tragedy; it is a tragedy for all of humanity.

For my family, for all the victims of the Holocaust and their descendants, and for the descendants of the non-Jewish victims of Nazi atrocities, the Bad Arolsen files will forever remain sacred family memorials. Here they will be able to recover the missing strands of their family histories and roots. And here, too, they will finally have access to the information that was for decades denied them – an injustice and cruelty that has yet to be fully accounted for.

Were it not for the Bad Arolsen documents, successive generations might find it impossible to imagine, let alone believe, that these horrendous crimes had ever been committed, and on such a massive scale. The human mind is simply not able to grasp this terrible truth: a nation transformed into a killing machine programmed to destroy millions of innocent human beings for no reason other than that they were different. The Bad Arolsen files tell this story, not only about the number of victims, but also about the suffering of each individual human being who perished in the camps.

The documents on deposit in Bad Arolsen must forever remind the world of the horrendous crimes the Nazi regime perpetrated, not in order to encourage hatred against today's Germany, which deserves admiration for its transformation from a killer nation into a truly democratic country, but, above all, as a perpetual reminder of the obligation that we and all future generations have to ensure that this terrible past is never repeated in any part of the world.

Thomas Buergenthal, January 2015

# Acknowledgements

This book does not have the usual publishing history. I wrote it in English, but it was first published in more than half a dozen other languages. While this is not a unique situation, it is rather rare unless political, religious or other reasons bar the publication of an author's books in his native country or language. That was certainly not true in my case. My problem, as I learned on more than one occasion from publishers in the United States and the United Kingdom, was that 'Holocaust books don't sell'. It is therefore ironic that this book was first published in Germany and that it remained on that country's bestseller list for quite a number of weeks.

It troubles me that some publishers in the English-speaking world assume that there is nothing more to be said about one of mankind's greatest human tragedies that their readers will want to read. If this assumption were to become a self-fulfilling prophecy, 'Never again!' would lapse into a slogan devoid of the meaning it is designed to convey. We cannot hope to prevent future genocides and crimes against humanity unless we seek to understand the truth about, and the causes of, the

Holocaust. Important insights about these questions can be gained not only from scholarly works, but also from the memoirs of those who lived through it. I am therefore most grateful to the publishers of this book, Profile Books in the United Kingdom and Little, Brown in the United States, for making my memoir available to the English-language reader.

My very special thanks and appreciation go to Andrew Franklin of Profile Books and to Tracy Behar of Little, Brown, for deciding to publish the book and for their insightful editorial suggestions. I also wish to express my admiration of Penny Daniel at Profile for so competently and pleasantly coordinating the publication effort between different parts of the world.

My agent, Eva Koralnik, of the Liepman Literary Agency in Zurich, Switzerland, deserves my appreciation for believing that my story should be published and for promoting its publication with enthusiasm and personal commitment.

Throughout the writing of this book I had the indispensable assistance of my secretary, Mrs Danielle Touffet-Okandeji. I am profoundly grateful to her for the intelligence, professional skill and, above all, helpful spirit with which she assisted me throughout its many drafts.

My wife, Peggy Buergenthal, has lived through each page of this book and its many revisions. She has been my most severe editor and critic. As a result, she has enabled me to write a book that benefited immensely from her loving support, deep understanding and creative editorial suggestions. In so many ways this is as much her book as it is mine.